ASSESSING STUDENTS
IN GROUPS

Experts in Assessment™

Series Editors

Thomas R. Guskey and Robert J. Marzano

Judith Arter, Jay McTighe
Scoring Rubrics in the Classroom: Using Performance Criteria for Assessing and Improving Student Performance

Jane M. Bailey, Thomas R. Guskey
Implementing Student-Led Conferences

Arthur L. Costa, Bena Kallick
Assessment Strategies for Self-Directed Learning

Gregory J. Cizek
Detecting and Preventing Classroom Cheating

Lorna M. Earl
Assessment As Learning: Using Classroom Assessment to Maximize Student Learning

Thomas R. Guskey, Jane M. Bailey
Developing Grading and Reporting Systems for Student Learning

David W. Johnson, Roger T. Johnson
Assessing Students in Groups: Promoting Group Responsibility and Individual Accountability

Edward Kifer
Large-Scale Assessment: Dimensions, Dilemmas, and Policy

Robert J. Marzano
Designing a New Taxonomy of Educational Objectives

James H. McMillan
Essential Assessment Concepts for Teachers and Administrators

Douglas B. Reeves
Holistic Accountability: Serving Students, Schools, and Community

Jeffrey K. Smith, Lisa F. Smith, Richard De Lisi
Natural Classroom Assessment: Designing Seamless Instruction and Assessment

ASSESSING STUDENTS IN GROUPS

PROMOTING GROUP RESPONSIBILITY AND INDIVIDUAL ACCOUNTABILITY

DAVID W. JOHNSON AND ROGER T. JOHNSON

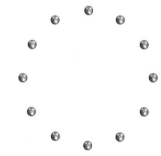

EXPERTS IN ASSESSMENT™

SERIES EDITORS
THOMAS R. GUSKEY AND ROBERT J. MARZANO

CORWIN PRESS
A Sage Publications Company
Thousand Oaks, California

For information:

Corwin Press
A Sage Publications Company
2455 Teller Road
Thousand Oaks, California 91320
www.corwinpress.com

Sage Publications Ltd.
6 Bonhill Street
London EC2A 4PU
United Kingdom

Sage Publications India Pvt. Ltd.
B-42, Panchsheel Enclave
Post Box 4109
New Delhi 110 017 India

Printed in the United States of America

Library of Congress Cataloging-in-Publication Data

Johnson, David W., 1940-
Assessing students in groups: Promoting group responsibility and individual accountability / by David W. Johnson and Roger T. Johnson.
    p. cm.
Includes bibliographical references and index.
ISBN 0-7619-3946-6 (cloth) – ISBN 0-7619-3947-4 (pbk.) 1. Group work in education—Evaluation. 2. Educational tests and measurements. I. Johnson, Roger T., 1938- II. Title.
LB1032.J592 2004
371.39'5–dc22   2003017595

This book is printed on acid-free paper.

06 10 9 8 7 6 5 4 3 2

Acquisitions Editor:	Rachel Livsey
Editorial Assistant:	Phyllis Cappello
Production Editor:	Kristen Gibson
Cover Designer:	Tracy E. Miller
Graphic Designer:	Lisa Miller
Typesetter:	C&M Digitals (P) Ltd.
Copy Editor:	Marilyn Power Scott
Proofreader:	Michele Lingre
Indexer:	Kay Dusheck

Contents

Series Editors' Introduction

Standards, assessment, accountability, and grading—these are the issues that dominated discussions of education in the 1990s. Today, they are at the center of every modern education reform effort. As educators turn to the task of implementing these reforms, they face a complex array of questions and concerns that little in their background or previous experience has prepared them to address. This series is designed to help in that challenging task.

In selecting the authors, we went to individuals recognized as true experts in the field. The ideas of these scholar-practitioners have already helped shape current discussions of standards, assessment, accountability, and grading. But equally important, their work reflects a deep understanding of the complexities involved in implementation. As they developed their books for this series, we asked them to extend their thinking, to push the edge, and to present new perspectives on what should be done and how to do it. That is precisely what they did. The books they crafted provide not only cutting-edge perspectives but also practical guidelines for successful implementation.

We have several goals for this series. First, that it be used by teachers, school leaders, policy makers, government officials, and all those concerned with these crucial aspects of education reform. Second, that it helps broaden understanding of the complex issues involved in standards, assessment, accountability, and grading. Third, that it leads to more thoughtful policies and programs. Fourth, and most important, that it helps accomplish the basic goal for which all reform initiatives are intended—namely, to enable all students to learn excellently and to gain the many positive benefits of that success.

Thomas R. Guskey
Robert J. Marzano
Series Editors

Preface

The purpose of this book is to provide you with a practical guide for (1) using learning groups for assessment purposes by making groups a context for individual and self-assessments and by assessing groups as a whole and (2) using learning groups in more effective ways. Read this book carefully and apply its content immediately and often in the classes you teach.

With the call for increased accountability of schools, there has been an emphasis on assessment. In this book we have presented a wide range of procedures for assessment in a meaningful and practical format that makes them easy to understand. Most of the more powerful and interesting assessment procedures require a group context. Learning groups provide the setting in which assessment procedures can be integrated with instruction and enhance the learning of each individual group member. With the use of learning groups, you can link what is taught with what is measured. The more skillfully instruction and assessment are interwoven in learning groups, the more students will learn and the more successful you will be as a teacher.

This book will be most useful when you read it within the context of a learning group. In reading and discussing this book with others, you are then in position to help each other implement new assessment procedures with real fidelity in your classrooms. Implementing new assessment procedures, as with all teaching, is like being in love—it always goes better with two.

We would like to thank Linda Johnson for her help and assistance. Her creativity and hard work are deeply appreciated.

About the Authors

David W. Johnson is a professor of educational psychology at the University of Minnesota. He is Co-Director of the Cooperative Learning Center. He is the recipient of the 2003 Distinguished Contributions of Applications of Psychology to Education and Training Award from the American Psychologist Association. He held the Emma M. Birkmaier Professorship in Educational Leadership at the University of Minnesota from 1994 to 1997 and the Libra Endowed Chair for Visiting Professor at the University of Maine in 1996-1997. He received his master's and doctoral degrees from Columbia University. He has authored over 400 research articles and book chapters. He is the author of over 40 books. He is a past editor of the *American Educational Research Journal.* He is the recipient of numerous awards for outstanding research and teaching from a wide variety of organizations. He is an organizational consultant to schools and businesses and is a psychotherapist.

Roger T. Johnson is a professor of curriculum and instruction at the University of Minnesota. He holds his doctoral degree from the University of California in Berkeley. He is the Co-Director of the Cooperative Learning Center. His public school teaching experience includes kindergarten through eighth grade instruction in self-contained classrooms, open schools, nongraded situations, cottage schools, and departmentalized (science) schools. He has consulted with schools throughout the world. He taught in the Harvard-Newton Intern Program as a master teacher. He was a curriculum developer with the Elementary Science Study in the Educational Development Center at Harvard University. For three summers, he taught classes in the British Primary Schools at the University of Sussex near Brighton, England. He has been honored with national awards from numerous organizations. He is the author of numerous research articles, book chapters, and books.

This book is dedicated to the thousands of teachers who have taken our training in cooperative learning and created classroom environments where students care about each other and each other's learning.

CHAPTER 1

The Power of Cooperative Groups

Sandy Koufax was one of the greatest pitchers in the history of baseball. Although he was naturally talented, he was also unusually well trained and disciplined. He was perhaps the only major-league pitcher whose fastball could be heard to hum. Opposing batters, instead of talking and joking around in the dugout, would sit quietly and listen for Koufax's fastball to hum. When it was their turn to bat, they were already intimidated. There was, however, a simple way for Koufax's genius to have been negated: by making the first author of this book his catcher. To be great, a pitcher needs an outstanding catcher (his great partner was Johnny Roseboro). David is such an unskilled catcher that Koufax would have had to throw the ball much slower for David to catch it. This would have deprived Koufax of his greatest weapon. Placing Roger, the other author, at a key defensive position in the infield or outfield would also have seriously affected Koufax's success. Sandy Koufax was not a great pitcher on his own. Only as part of a team could Koufax achieve greatness. In baseball and in the classroom, it takes a team effort. Extraordinary achievement comes more often from cooperative groups than from isolated individuals competing with each other or working alone.

To understand the power of groups, it is first necessary to define instruction and assessment. We then discuss the power of groups in assessment and evaluation, the conditions needed for valid and reliable assessment, where groups should be used for instruction and assessment, and eight steps of using groups for assessment.

The Interrelationships
Between Instruction and Assessment

To use the power of groups for assessment, it is first necessary to define the interrelationships between instruction and assessment. **Instruction** may be defined as the structuring of situations in ways that help students change, through learning. **Learning** is change within a student that is brought about by instruction. Teachers are responsible for instructing students to create learning. To determine the impact of instruction on learning, assessment procedures are required. **Assessment** involves collecting information about the quality or quantity of a change in a student or group. **Evaluation** may be defined as judging the merit, value, or desirability of a measured performance. Assessment should be continuous, as it is an essential aspect of instruction and learning. Evaluation, on the other hand, may be done only occasionally, as it is not necessary for instruction or learning but exists for other purposes. You can assess without evaluation, but you cannot evaluate without assessment. The quality of the assessment largely determines the quality of the evaluation.

Assessment may be conducted on individual, group, classroom, school, district, state, or national levels. **Individual assessment** involves collecting information about the quality or quantity of a change in a student, while **group assessment** is collecting information about the quality or quantity of a change in a group as a whole. Assessments may be conducted not only by the teacher but also by classmates and oneself. **Peer assessment** occurs when peers collect information about the quality or quantity of change in a student. **Self-assessment** occurs when a person collects information about the quality or quantity of a change in himself or herself. All four types of assessment (individual, group, peer, self) are necessary to maximize the learning of each individual student. While a great deal has been written about assessing the learning of individuals, much less is known about the assessment of groups and the use of peer and self-assessments to increase student learning.

Instruction, learning, assessment, and evaluation are so intertwined that it is difficult to separate them. Teachers plan instructional activities, students participate in them, the amount of learning is assessed, feedback is given to students, both students and teachers reflect on the results, and the processes of instruction and learning are modified to make them more effective, and occasionally, students' learning is evaluated (see Figure 1.1).

Transfer of Learning to Assessment Situations

Assessment has traditionally focused on individual-to-individual transfer of learning. Students worked in isolation from classmates (in

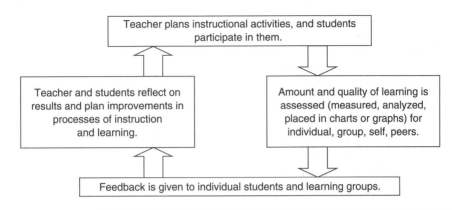

Figure 1.1   Interrelationships Among Instruction, Learning, Assessment, and Evaluation

either competitive or individualistic learning situations) and were given individual tests to assess their achievement. This practice was based on the assumption that individual assessment requires individual learning. This is a misconception. Group-to-individual transfer has been repeatedly demonstrated to be superior to individual-to-individual transfer (Johnson & Johnson, 1989). The purpose of cooperative learning groups is to ensure that all members learn and are, therefore, better able to perform on subsequent individual assessment measures as a result of their group experience.

Whose Learning Is It? Assisted Learning, Assisted Assessments, and Equalizing the Playing Field

Assessments have traditionally focused on unassisted student learning. Students were supposed to complete work by themselves (i.e., without the assistance of others). While there are assessment situations in which students should work alone, this does not mean that student learning should be unassisted. During learning situations, students should be exposed to sources of help and assistance, such as teachers, curriculum materials, resource experts, classmates, parents, private tutors, the Internet, educational programs on television or video, and so forth. All school learning is assisted and promoted by the instructional efforts of a wide variety of individuals within and outside of the school.

In learning situations, each student should receive the maximal amount of assistance possible. Thus the teacher should provide as much academic help and support as time allows. The curriculum materials and the instructional technology should be the best that the school district can afford. Parents should be enlisted to help students with homework and to provide a tutor when a student needs one. Classmates and friends should be expected to provide as much academic help and support as they can. In the classroom, cooperative learning groups are used to provide the help and support that each student needs to maximize his or her learning.

In some assessment situations, certain students receive more help, assistance, and support than do other students. This raises the question, Whose work is it? and presents a potential threat to the validity of interpretations about individual scores. It may be unclear what a specific student can do individually. Homework is an example. Some students may turn in homework they have done themselves. Other students may seek out the teacher, receive help and assistance, and turn in teacher-assisted homework. Some students may get help from their parents or from a privately hired tutor and turn in parent-assisted or tutor-assisted homework. Other students may complete homework with their friends and turn in friend-assisted homework. Some students may have access to information on the internet and even enter chat-rooms in which help doing their homework is obtained; they hand in internet-assisted homework. When it comes to homework assessment, students who do not receive help and assistance are at a disadvantage. Communities in which parents are highly educated professionals, for example, may produce student work superior to that produced by students in districts with less educated and wealthy parents.

The disadvantage some students face because they have fewer or lower-quality sources of assistance than do classmates may be equalized through the use of cooperative learning groups. In cooperative learning groups, students who have access to the internet can share what they have found with their groupmates, students who have private tutors can pass on the tutoring, students who received extra help from the teacher can share what they learned, and so forth. Beginning each class period with a cooperative base group meeting in which students go over the homework and share what they have learned in completing it, for example, provides an opportunity to level the playing field and let each student benefit from the special resources and sources of assistance available to their classmates. Without cooperative learning groups, the classroom playing field may never be level.

The issue of assisted assessments is avoided when assessment procedures lead to individual performances on demand. For example, a student can write a series of compositions during a school year, all of which go through an editing process within the classroom (peer editing), the family (parent or sibling editing), or with a tutor (tutor editing). While these compositions reflect what the student is capable of (given the editing and feedback from classmates, parents, tutors, and teachers), it does not reflect how well the student can write on demand. The teacher, therefore, may wish to give a test in which students are given a certain amount of class time (such as thirty minutes) to write an essay. The extent to which the writing skills learned transfer to new writing demands can then be assessed.

Instruction, learning, assessment, and evaluation are all interrelated. Assessment can focus on either individuals or groups, and assessments can be conducted by the teacher, classmates, or oneself. While assessments have often focused on individual-to-individual transfer of learning and unassisted student performances, assessment is enriched by group-to-individual transfer, and assessed learning and assessments help level the playing field so that all students have an equal opportunity to perform well. Assessments can be truly enriched by the power of learning groups.

Integrating Instruction and Assessment

A common misperception is that instruction and assessment are separate activities. In fact, instruction is considerably enhanced when it is integrated with assessment. Six of the interdependent ways that assessment can be integrated into instruction are as follows: First, assessment can require a systematic review of what is being learned. Such assessments can result in students engaging in the cognitive rehearsal of what is being learned. Second, assessment activities can require the integration of what is being learned with previous learning. Third, assessment activities can facilitate the creation of conceptual frameworks that provide organization and meaning to what is being learned. Fourth, assessment can require higher-level reasoning about what is being learned. This enhances the quality of the learning experience and enriches subsequent group discussions. Fifth, assessments can require a reconceptualization of what is being learned that integrates it into expanded cognitive frameworks. By asking students to use what they have learned in new ways, the result can be a rethinking of what has been learned and connecting it with other conceptual frameworks. Sixth, assessments can require students to extend their learning to new situations and problems. Transfer of learning is enhanced the more varied the situations in which students use what they are learning. Assessments can provide such varied situations. All of these ways of integrating assessment into instruction may be more effective when students are learning in groups and can discuss the results of the assessments with groupmates and then use the results of the assessment in the next phase of the learning activity. Refer often to the Checklist for Integrating Assessment Into Instruction as you make your lesson plans.

Checklist for Integrating Assessment Into Instruction

1. Systematically review what is being learned.

2. Integrate what is being learned into a conceptual framework.

3. Create conceptual frameworks within which to organize current learning.

4. Move reasoning about what is being learned to higher levels.

5. Require a reconceptualization of what is being learned.

6. Require an extension of what is being learned.

Power of Groups

The New York Yankees has been one of the best teams in baseball for most of its history (Sternberg & Grigorenko, 2000). There was a brief period of time, however, when the team was losing. This period occurred after the team's owner spent large amounts of money to hire some of the best baseball players in the world. These prima donnas could not work together, as each one tried to be the hero of each game. Despite the star players, the team was striking out. The same has happened in academic departments. One of the great English departments in the United States hired a collection of superstar professors (significantly increasing its reputation), but when the professors could not work together, the department's reputation plummeted.

Examples like this illustrate that in considering the effectiveness of a school or teacher, the degree to which individuals work together to promote each other's achievement and productivity largely determines effectiveness. The success of any one student or teacher cannot be separated from the success of the class or school as a whole. Any baseball or football player can tell you that although individual members make important contributions, their collective teamwork is the key to success. Unfortunately, the academic culture of the many schools tends to be so competitive or individualistic that teams are discouraged, despite the reality that most of the serious research is done in teams. This is true despite the fact that in the real world of work, teamwork is becoming more and more important. As science advances, for example, there is less and less that any one individual can do alone to make any substantial advance in research and knowledge. Much research can be accomplished only as teams work effectively together. Thus both working as part of a team and coordinating the efforts of multiple teams are becoming more and more important to advancing knowledge, scientific success, and the success of almost any employee in any job. If schools are to be microcosms of the real world, teamwork has to be promoted throughout each school day.

Inevitability of Groups

The power of groups is reflected in their inevitability and ubiquitousness. Whether teachers encourage it or not, students will form groups. It is what humans do. No matter what historical period, no matter what culture, no matter what geographical area humans live in, people form groups and resist the dissolution of their groups (Gardner, Pickett, & Brewer, 2000; Manstead & Hewstone, 1995). There is a substantial survival advantage to joining groups and maintaining one's memberships in groups (Baumeister & Leary, 1995). Groups are better able to hunt for and grow food, find mates, and care for children. We are born into a group called the family, without which we would not survive the first few minutes, weeks, or years of our lives. We learn, work, worship, and play in groups. Our life is filled with groups from the moment of our birth to the moment of our death. Groups are so central to our lives that it is difficult to contemplate humans ever existing without them. If a being from outer space conducted a study of the people of earth, group membership would probably be the dominant characteristic noted. All of this means that groups are pervasive, and students will form groups no matter whether the teacher wants them to or not.

Groups Influence Behavior

The power of groups is reflected in the impact they have on students' actions. The groups we belong to largely determine our behavior (Johnson & F. Johnson, 2003). Groups provide information that helps us resolve ambiguity about the nature of our social world. It is within our family and peer groups that we are socialized into ways of behaving and thinking, where we are educated and taught to have certain perspectives on our world and ourselves. Groups are an important part of our identities, helping us define who we are (e.g., people wear shirts, hats, pins, and other items with the name of one of their groups on it). Groups establish social norms about what is and is not acceptable behavior. Groups influence what we value and what we aspire to achieve. The family we grew up in, the friends we have made and kept, the schools we attended, the organizations in which we work all influence our actions. It is the groups to which we belong to that give us faith and hope, determine how we perceive the world, shape what we aspire to and value, and influence what we consider appropriate and inappropriate behavior. The groups we belong to influence what clothes we wear, what music we listen to, the slang and expressions we use, and the fads we follow, and they even determine how we perceive ourselves. The degree to which students value education, strive to achieve, and care about grades is largely influenced by the groups to which they belong. Groups influence almost every aspect of our behavior and lives.

Groups Enhance Achievement

The power of groups is reflected in their impact on individual achievement. Just as groups are central to every human culture, they are central to education. Communities send children to be educated in large groups known as schools. Schools divide students into smaller groups called "classes," and classes are divided into learning groups. Students tend to achieve and retain more when they work in cooperative learning groups than when they work competitively or individualistically (Johnson & Johnson, 1989). Benefits from group work include decreased student absenteeism and increased student preparation and effort (Dinan, 1995). Atkinson and Raynor (1974), theorists and researchers on achievement motivation, stated, "Achievement is a 'we' thing, not a 'me' thing, always the product of many heads and hands" (p. xi). Despite the North American myth of the remarkable individual who achieves great things in isolation from others, in business and industry, family life and parenting, communities and societies, and all other aspects of life, there is nothing quite so creative and productive as a cooperative group (Bennis & Biederman, 1997). It is groups that leave behind creations such as the atom bomb, a new computer, a family of cartoon characters, a walk on the moon, or a painted ceiling of the Sistine Chapel. The more sophisticated and technological the society, the more the coordinated contributions of many talented people are required to solve urgent problems. Building a global business, mapping the genetic structure of a disease, improving the human immune system—all are beyond the efforts of even the most gifted and energetic individual. It takes teams working together to achieve such goals. The history of the world is the history of extraordinary collaborations, where a group accomplishes much more than talented people working alone. Margaret Mead (as quoted in Bennis & Biederman, 1997) suggested that such groups be called, "sapiential circles."

This power of collaboration is also true in the classroom. Students working alone can complete simple assignments, learn simple procedures and information, and engage in well-learned behaviors. When new and complex knowledge and skills need to be mastered or extraordinary effort is needed, however, learning groups are necessary.

There are too many advantages to using groups in education to discuss them all, but here are some of the biggest: Groups can raise individuals' levels of aspirations. Groups can inspire individuals to achieve beyond their wildest expectations. Groups can give individuals insights and understandings that could never be achieved alone. Groups can ferment creativity and the unlocking of potential. Groups can change the way people perceive the world and the reality of their lives. Groups can provide variety, entertainment, and fun. If students were required to work alone all day, classroom life could be lonely, dull, boring, and alienating.

Groups Enhance Relationships

The power of groups is also reflected in their impact on interpersonal relationships (Johnson & Johnson, 1989). There are few life experiences more destructive than the absence of positive relationships with others, especially one's peers. All students need to have peers who know them well and like and respect them as individuals. Cooperative experiences, compared with competitive and individualistic experiences, result in more positive and supportive relationships (Johnson & Johnson, 1989). More friendships form and fewer students remain isolated when cooperative groups are used.

Groups Enhance Psychological Health

The power of groups is reflected in their impact of students' mental health (Johnson & Johnson, 1989). Membership in any group confers informational and emotional benefits to the member, including increased information resources, emotional resources, and the opportunity to take on different roles and identities. These processes are so powerful that people's mental health status is positively associated with the number of groups they belong to (Johnson & Johnson, 1989).

Groups Enhance Social Skills

The power of groups is reflected in their impact on the development of interpersonal and small-group skills (Johnson & F. Johnson, 2003). Developing teamwork skills (such as communication, division of labor, generosity in giving credit, constructive criticism, caring, sharing, support of others, and team spirit) can be at least as important to future career success as the development of individual academic skills. Therefore, students should be explicitly helped to develop interpersonal and small-group skills rather than leaving the development of these skills to chance. In fact, an exclusive emphasis on individual academic learning can retard instruction and decrease learning. As Sternberg and Grigorenko (2000) note, there never really was or is a Lone Ranger, so why pretend otherwise?

Groups Help Make Assessments Meaningful

The power of groups is reflected in their impact on the perceived meaning of assessments. Involving students in assessment increases the meaning they attach to the assessments (Johnson & Johnson, 1996, 2002). Even high-stakes assessments can be resisted when they are perceived to be meaningless. Even low-stakes assessments can be entered into with great enthusiasm and effort when they are perceived to be meaningful. Assessments are perceived by students to be meaningful (1) when they have a significant purpose (such as contributing to the learning of groupmates and the common good); (2) when they consist of procedures, criteria, and rubrics that are clearly understood; and (3) when the results provide a clear direction for increasing the quality of learning and instruction. Unless the purpose is perceived to be significant, the procedures are clearly understood, and the results are perceived to be useful and relevant, the individuals whose performances are being assessed will not do their best and will not facilitate the assessment process.

Groups Provide the Framework for Involving Students in Making Assessments

The power of groups is reflected in their impact on student involvement in assessments. No matter how desirable an assessment procedure is, if it is time consuming and complex, teachers cannot use it. **Manageability** includes whether the available resources are adequate for the requirements of the assessment procedure and whether the value of the information obtained is worth the expenditure of the resources (Johnson & Johnson, 1996, 2002). Resources are required for (1) setting the learning goals in a way that induces student commitment to achieve the goals; (2) selecting the procedures to be used (such as tests, compositions, portfolios, projects, observations); (3) collecting and analyzing the data from diagnostic, formative, and summative assessments; and (d) recording and reporting results (includes charting the results and reporting activities such as student-led conferences). New learning goals are then set: either remediation to bring a student's performance up to the criteria for mastery or new goals for the next instructional unit.

The major issue in managing assessments is teacher time. Most teachers do not have much time to conduct assessments. Swain and Swain (1999), for example, note that in America, almost all of the official working time of teachers is committed to the classroom instruction of students. Teachers in the United States devote more hours to instruction and supervision of students each week and have longer required workweeks than in any other developed, industrialized country, including the nations with six-day weeks, such as Japan and Switzerland. Consequently, most of the assessment activities must be done at night or on weekends. Swain and Swain conclude that teachers who spend twelve minutes to plan for each class session and nine minutes per week to assess each student's work have no choice but to work sixty hours a week or more. If teachers work forty-five hours a week, they will have six minutes to plan for each class session and three minutes per week to assess each student's work. Obviously, three minutes a week is not enough time to conduct any sort of meaningful assessment. The result may be the use of inadequate assessment procedures. Swain and Swain note that if it takes a teacher fifteen or twenty hours outside of school to grade essays from an assignment, then teachers may decide to assign fewer essays.

Time constraints can prohibit the use of many of the most effective and helpful assessment procedures. Teachers simply do not have the time to use them without help and assistance. If the more creative and effective assessment procedures are to be used, teachers need additional sources of labor. The most natural sources of help for teachers are students. Students are an ideal source of help because (1) they are always present in the classroom; (2) student commitment to implement the results of an assessment is greater when they collect, analyze, and interpret the data themselves; and (3) students may often learn more from conducting assessments than they do from receiving assessments. For these and many other reasons, it is often advisable (and necessary) to involve students in learning assessment rubrics and using them to reflect on and assess their own and their classmates' work.

Groups Empower Teachers to Enlarge the Scope of Assessments

The power of groups is reflected in the ways it enables teachers to increase the scope of assessments. Having students help conduct assessments allows teachers to do the following:

1. Provide students with powerful learning experiences that increase their achievement. Assessing the accuracy, quantity, and quality of their own and classmates' work tends to make the assessment and reporting processes important learning experiences. In addition, when students conduct assessments of classmates' work, they learn the criteria and rubrics used in assessment more thoroughly, thus developing internal guidelines and greater understanding of how their work should be completed. Involving students in the assessment process can result in greater integration of assessment and instruction.

2. Conduct more frequent assessments. Having students assess each other's work significantly increases the frequency with which assessments can be conducted as well as the amount of work that may be assigned.

3. Assess a wider variety of outcomes. Outcomes that are ignored because they are too labor intensive to assess or require frequent and continuous monitoring may be included in an assessment plan when students are available to help. When students work together, covert reasoning and problem-solving processes, social skills, attitudes and values, and work habits may be made overt so that they can be assessed and improved.

4. Use more modalities in assessing students' work. In addition to assessing each other's reading and writing, students can observe each other presenting, performing cognitive and social skills, demonstrating higher-level reasoning procedures, using visuals such as graphs and illustrations, and even acting out or role playing aspects of the content being learned. This considerably enriches student assessment.

5. Use more sources of information in making assessments. Student involvement makes self and peer assessments available as well as teacher assessments. Self, peer, and teacher assessments can then be coordinated and integrated. Students as well as teachers can communicate the results of assessments to interested audiences.

6. Reduce sources of bias. There are at least two sources of bias in classroom assessments. The first is the inherent bias in making reading and writing prerequisites for revealing knowledge or engaging in a performance. The second is potential teacher bias due to such factors as neatness of handwriting (Sweedler-Brown, 1992) and teachers' perceptions of students' behavior (Bennett, Gottesman, Rock, & Cerullo, 1993; Hills, 1991). The more students assess each other's work, the less the potential there is for these biases.

7. Create classmate social support systems for remediation and enrichment activities. The limits on teacher time prevent teachers from constantly monitoring each student's efforts to learn and requires that only a sample be assessed. In small cooperative groups, classmates can continuously monitor each other's activities and provide both academic and personal support.

8. Create opportunities to assess group as well as individual outcomes. There are scientific, dramatic, or creative projects that may only be done by groups.

Groups Mediate the Impact of Evaluation

The power of groups is reflected in the ways the impact of evaluation is mediated. Students may be asked to perform on well-learned tasks and on new, complex tasks (see Figure 1.2). Whether they work in groups or are evaluated as individuals has considerable influence on their performance. Even the mere presence of others observing us work when our individual performance is being evaluated tends to improve our performance on well-learned tasks (Johnson & F. Johnson, 2003). This is known as the **social facilitation effect.** Social facilitation theorists conclude that working with other people when we are not being evaluated creates mild physiological arousal that energizes us to engage in the work and causes us to become particularly alert and vigilant, which results in our doing a good job (Zajonc, 1980).

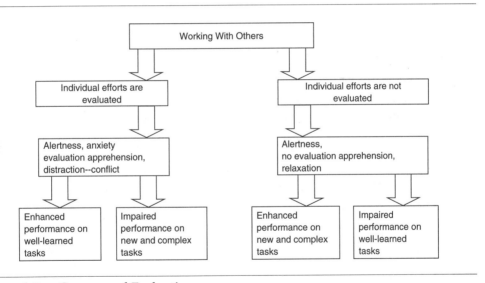

Figure 1.2   Groups and Evaluation

We tend to become more physically energized when we work with other people, and we know that we are going to be individually evaluated (more so than when we work alone), and the increase in psychological arousal makes it easier for us to engage in a dominant response but harder to do something complex or learn something new. When we are apprehensive about being evaluated, however, working with others may result in evaluation apprehension and anxiety, which interfere with performance on new and complex tasks. The presence of others may create cognitive conflict over whether to attend to the evaluators or to the task, which distracts us from the task at hand and lowers our performance, especially on complex and new tasks (Baron, 1986).

Thus on new and complex tasks, our performance is higher when we work in the presence of others but are not evaluated. When individuals are not worried about being evaluated and they work together, they tend to be more relaxed and thus do better on difficult tasks (Jackson & Williams, 1985). When we are not going to be individually evaluated, working with others tends to relax us and reduce evaluation apprehension, enabling us to perform higher on complex tasks and learn new things; but under certain conditions, working with others may result in less effort on well-learned tasks.

Groups Enable the Assessment of a Wider Range of Outcomes

The power of groups is reflected in the range of outcomes that may be assessed. Most outcomes of instruction can be assessed either individually or in groups. Cognitive outcomes, such as domain-specific knowledge (declarative, procedural, schematic, and strategic knowledge in broad domains, such as humanities, social sciences, science), learning skills (such as comprehending, problem solving, decision making), reasoning with or applying knowledge in problem solving (verbal, quantitative, and spatial reasoning), and learning about one's learning, can sometimes be best measured individually and at other times best measured in groups. Personal and social outcomes, such as empathy, caring, compassion, and self-understanding, may be measured through individual questionnaires, but if teachers wish to assess students' abilities to engage in such behaviors, a group setting is necessary. In today's discussions about assessing learning and national, state, and local accountability systems, the desired outcomes of education are almost always confined to individual measurement of cognitive outcomes at the expense of personal, social, and civic outcomes.

Groups allow for the assessment of a wide range of outcomes that cannot be assessed when individuals work alone. Examples are as follows (Johnson & Johnson, 1996, 2002):

1. In groups, members give oral explanations, which tend to result in higher-level reasoning, deeper-level understanding, and long-term retention. These outcomes are often difficult to assess. To determine what students truly understand, it is necessary to make covert cognitive processes overt. Teachers listen to the group members working together and can determine the level of understanding students have

of the material they are studying. Without cooperative groups in which students are explaining to each other what they are learning, such assessment is not possible.

2. In groups, members may disagree with each other and challenge each other's conclusions and reasoning. Such intellectual conflict, when it is managed constructively, fuels higher-level reasoning, divergent thinking, creativity, and long-term retention (Johnson & Johnson, 1995c). Creative problem solving is especially enhanced by intellectual conflict among groupmates. The ways in which intellectual conflicts are managed and the creativeness of arriving at a conclusion can only be assessed in a group. Without cooperative groups in which students engage in intellectual conflicts, such assessment is not possible.

3. In groups, assessment can involve modalities other than reading and writing. Students who have trouble reading can learn assigned material orally. The discussion inherent in groupwork deemphasizes reading ability and emphasizes oral competencies. Groups provide an arena in which oral examinations on students' knowledge, reasoning, and problem solving can take place, and immediate feedback and remediation may be given.

4. In groups, social skills may be assessed. While a group works, communication must be effective, leadership must be provided, trust must be built and maintained, decisions must be made, conflicts must be resolved, and so forth. Such social skills cannot be assessed when students are working alone. Without cooperative groups, the assessment of social skills may not be possible.

5. In groups, attitudes and values may be more apparent and easier to assess. Working in cooperative learning groups tends to result in more positive attitudes toward learning and more prosocial values than does learning competitively or individualistically. Attitudes and values are reflected in behavior in interaction among group members and therefore are more open to assessment. Without cooperative groups in which students actualize their attitudes and values through the way they interact, such assessment may not be possible.

6. In groups, work habits may be more apparent and easier to assess.

7. In groups, civic outcomes, such as taking initiative, demonstrating social responsibility, engaging in civic projects, and so forth, can be measured.

8. In groups, a wide variety of skills and competencies (such as problem solving, interacting effectively with diverse peers, use of technology, writing, and speaking) can be assessed.

See Figure 1.3 for a comparison of group and individual assessment.

Characteristic	Individual Assessment	Group Assessment
Assessor	Teacher	Teacher, peer, self
Outcomes assessed	Cognitive	Cognitive, competencies, personal, social, civic, attitudes, values, work habits
Source of feedback	Teacher	Teacher, peers, self
Frequency of assessments	Limited by teacher time	Limited by teacher and students' time
Modalities	One	Many
Social comparison	Limited opportunity	Continuous opportunity
Instruments, procedures	Primarily objective tests	Objective and essay tests, compositions and presentations, observing, interviews, enactment of social skills.
Peer influences	Neutral or away from achievement	Toward achievement

Figure 1.3   Group and Individual Assessment

Conditions for Valid and Reliable Assessments

For assessments to be valid and reliable, the assessor must accurately perceive the assessee and the assessee's performances. The accuracy of perceptions is influenced not only by the validity and reliability of the assessment instruments but also by such factors as the trust level between the assessor and the assessee and the openness and honesty of the communications. The greater the trust level and the more open and honest the communications between the assessor and the assessee, the more valid and reliable the assessments will tend to be. The assessors typically are teachers, classmates, and oneself.

Accurate perceptions, trust, and open communication are characteristics of a cooperative relationship, which also promotes many other behaviors that facilitate accurate assessments. Competition, on the other hand, promotes misperceptions of each other and each other's behavior, distrusting and untrustworthy actions, closed and inaccurate communication, and many other behaviors that interfere with and obstruct accurate assessments. Individualistic efforts tend to result in behaviors similar to competition. To understand how to conduct accurate assessments, therefore, it is necessary to understand how to build and maintain cooperative relationships. This is the focus of Chapter 2.

Where Groups Should Be Used

Instruction groups may be used in almost any lesson, subject area, grade, and curriculum unit. In deciding whether groups should be used in a lesson, however, teachers may use several guidelines. One set of guidelines involves the nature of the lesson. Groups should be used when (1) the instructional goals indicate their use, (2) there are limited materials, (3) the task is complex, (4) new material is being learned, (5) multiple perspectives are being studied, (6) creativity is required, (7) the task involves solving a problem, and (8) there are divisible responsibilities.

The second set of guidelines involves the findings of research. Groups should be used when (1) achievement, retention, deeper-level understanding, and higher-level reasoning are important; (2) intrinsic motivation, continuing motivation, and achievement motivation are important; (3) positive interpersonal relationships among students, especially diverse students, are important; (4) students need social support both academically and personally from their classmates and the teacher; (5) students' self-esteem and self-efficacy are important; (6) students' social skills, interpersonal competencies, and abilities to work as parts of teams are important; and (7) students' general psychological health is important.

The third set of guidelines involves tradition, that is, how you have structured the lesson in the past. If you have traditionally used groups for this lesson, then do so again.

Despite the many advantages of using groups, many teachers do not do so. Why is the power of groups ignored (see "Why the Power of Cooperative Groups Is Ignored).

Eight Steps of Using Groups for Assessment

Given that valid and reliable assessments depend on cooperative relationships among students and faculty and that learning groups may be used in almost any lesson, the use of learning groups in assessment needs to be discussed. There are eight steps in using groups for assessment:

Why the Power of Cooperative Groups Is Ignored

Directions: Consider the five sources of resistance to using cooperative groups given below. Rate yourself from "1" to "5" on each source.

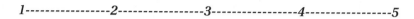

1----------------2----------------3----------------4----------------5

Low	**Middle**	**High**
Not a concern of mine	Somewhat a concern	Consistently and strongly a concern

	The Causes of the Missed Opportunities to Capitalize on the Power of Groups
	1. **Belief that isolated work is the natural order of the world.** Such myopic focus blinds educators to the realization that no one person could have built a cathedral, achieved America's independence from England, or created a supercomputer.
	2. **Resistance to taking responsibility for others.** Many educators do not easily (1) take responsibility for the performance of colleagues or (2) let colleagues assume responsibility for their work. The same educators may resist letting students take responsibility for each other's learning.
	3. **Confusion about what makes groups work.** Many educators may not know the difference between cooperative learning groups and traditional groupwork.
	4. **Fear that they cannot use groups effectively to enhance learning and improve teaching.** Not all groups work. Most adults have had personal experiences with very ineffective and inefficient committees, task forces, and clubs and know firsthand how bad groups can be. When many educators weigh the potential power of learning groups against the possibility of failure, they choose to play it safe and stick with the status quo of isolated work.
	5. **Concern about time and effort required to change.** Using cooperative learning requires educators to apply what is known about effective groups in a disciplined way. Learning how to do so and engaging in such disciplined action may seem daunting.

First, teachers need to realize that groups have powerful effects not only on achievement and other instructional outcomes but also on assessments. That is the focus of this chapter.

Second, not all groups are powerful, and not all groups enhance instruction and assessment. There is more to making groups effective than seating students together and telling them they are a team. Poorly structured groups may be at best inefficient and at worst destructive to members. To be effective, learning groups need to be cooperative, with five basic elements (i.e., positive interdependence, individual accountability, promotive interaction, social skills, and group processing) carefully structured in the learning situation. Any assignment in any subject area may be structured cooperatively. There are three types of cooperative learning groups: formal cooperative learning, informal cooperative learning, and cooperative base groups. Each may be used to enhance the quality of assessments and integrate instruction and assessment. These are discussed more fully in Chapter 2.

Third, teachers make assessment plans that include cooperative learning groups as the setting in which the assessment is organized. While students learn in cooperative learning groups, teachers may assess individuals, groups, or both. The teacher decides which specific processes and outcomes (e.g., knowledge, reasoning processes, skills and competencies, attitudes and values, work habits) will be assessed, the sequence of the instructional tasks, the assessment procedures (tests, observations, portfolios, reports, and so forth), and the purpose of assessments (diagnostic, formative, or summative). Groups can provide immediate remediation and enrichment thus integrating instruction and assessment. Assessment plans are discussed in Chapter 3.

Fourth, groups are used as the setting in which each member is assessed as an individual. The basic purpose of a cooperative group is to make each member a stronger individual in his or her own right. There is a pattern to classroom life that can be summarized as learn it in a group, perform it alone. Most assessments begin, therefore, with the teacher using groups to more accurately assess each group member as a separate individual. Groups are necessary for the assessment of many individual outcomes. There are many individual performances (such as mastery of social skills, singing in harmony, playing an instrument in concert with others, passing the ball to a teammate in basketball, giving an encouraging remark to a groupmate who is too shy to participate, expanding on a classmate's idea, giving good explanations, summarizing and integrating the views of others, criticizing the reasoning of another person, and so forth) that can only be assessed within a group setting. Within learning groups, learning goals are set for each member. Assessment procedures are then used, such as individual tests, questionnaires, interviews, and observations. The teacher may use the results of the individual assessments to structure the agenda for the next group session, and the group may use the individual assessments to provide remediation and further instruction of each member. Using groups to assess individuals is discussed in Chapter 4.

Fifth, on many assignments, groups produce a product that should be assessed. Obviously, group assessment cannot take place without groups. Group assessment involves having students work in small groups to complete a lesson, project, or test while a teacher or group members (or both) measure the level of performance of the group as a whole. There are many desired outcomes of school activities that can only be assessed if students work in groups and are assessed at a group level, such as performing a play, winning a basketball or volleyball game, or the making a video. Science experiments, dramatic or musical productions, team sports, history field projects and many, many more assignments may result in group products that are assessed as wholes. When group projects are assigned, problem-based learning used, and case studies are discussed, the result of the group effort is assessed. How to do so is discussed in Chapter 5.

Sixth, groups are necessary for peer assessments. Obviously, if students are to assess each other's learning, they have to work together so that each person's learning processes and quality and quantity of actual learning can be observed and understood. Peers may be the source of the most complete, accurate, and helpful assessments and feedback. The more students work together and the more cooperative the situation, the more accurate, fair, and insightful peer assessments will be. While teachers may sample students' behavior, groupmates continuously monitor each other's work and performances. Assessing each other's work increases the learning of each assessor, allows for more frequent assessments to take place, allows for the assessment of a wider variety of outcomes, allows for the use of more modalities in assessment and thereby reduces the bias inherent in making reading and writing prerequisites for assessment, allows for the use of more sources of information, reduces potential teacher bias in assessment, and creates peer social support systems for remediation and enrichment. Peer assessments are the focus of Chapter 6.

Seventh, the teacher may structure self-assessments based on the experiences of working cooperatively with classmates. Engaging in self-assessment requires a comparison process (either with a person's past performances, preset criteria, or the performance of similar others) and procedures for gathering information about such things as one's performances, actions, emotions, intentions, and values. All three types of comparisons are helpful, but it is the comparison of one's performances with the performances of others than is often most informative. Self-assessments, therefore, are much more reliable and accurate when a person has been working cooperatively with others. Self-assessment is discussed in Chapter 7.

Last, the teacher may create group situations for assessment purposes, such as the use of role-playing situations, simulations, and academic controversies. This is discussed in Chapter 8.

Summary

Instruction, learning, assessment, and evaluation all take place in a network of interpersonal relationships in which people work cooperatively to maximize their learning and the learning of classmates. Instruction is aimed at producing learning that is then assessed and evaluated. Assessment should be continuous, but evaluation should be done only occasionally. The teacher plans instructional activities, the resulting learning is assessed, feedback is given to individual students and learning groups, students and teachers reflect on the results, and the processes of instruction and learning are modified to make them more effective; and occasionally, students' learning is evaluated. The effectiveness of instruction is considerably enhanced when assessment is integrated into the instructional activities. The use of learning groups has powerful effects on this process.

Assessment has traditionally focused on individual-to-individual transfer of learning and unassisted individual learning, which are reflected in both competitive and individualistic learning. The power of groups for both instruction and assessment has been relatively ignored to date. Students will form groups despite how learning is structured as forming groups is an essential part of human nature. Not only are groups inevitable and ubiquitous, they enhance achievement, positive relationships with classmates, psychological health, and social skills. In addition, learning groups help make assessment meaningful, provide the framework for involving students in the assessment process, and enable the teacher to conduct more frequent assessments, assess a wider variety of outcomes, use more modalities in assessing students' work, use more sources of information in making assessments, reduce biases in assessment, create support systems, and assess groups as well as the individual members. Groups mediate the impact of evaluation so that when students working in learning groups are being evaluated, they perform better on well-learned tasks, but when they are not being evaluated, they perform better on new and complex tasks. A much wider range of outcomes can be assessed when learning groups are used. Last, groups have powerful effects on students' behavior through socialization and development, social influence, and attitude and value development. In short, the use of learning groups opens the classroom to assessment potentials that many schools have not dreamed of.

When learning groups are used for instruction and assessment, the validity and reliability of the assessments increase as the relationship between the teacher and the students and among the students becomes more cooperative and less competitive or individualistic. Learning groups may be used in any lesson, but they are especially apt when the task is complex and material is new, when positive relationships and social skills are important as well as achievement, and when it is traditional to do so.

There are eight steps in using learning groups for assessment purposes. Teachers should recognize the power of groups, know how to structure groups to ensure that they are cooperative, make an assessment plan, use groups to help in individual assessments, assess the groups as a whole, use peer assessments, use self-assessments, and create group situations in which targeted competencies and skills may be assessed. Each one of these steps is the subject of a chapter in this book.

CHAPTER 2

Structuring Productive Groups

There is a power to working in groups. A group of staff and trustees at the Bronx Educational Services shaped the first nationally recognized adult literacy school. A group of citizens in Harlem founded and operated the first Little League there in over forty years. Motorola used small manufacturing groups to produce the world's lightest, smallest, and highest-quality cellular phones (with only a few hundred parts versus over a thousand for the competition). Ford became America's most profitable car company in 1990 on the strength of the use of small groups to build its Taurus model. It was groups that built the pyramids, constructed the Temple of Artemis at Ephesus, created the Colossus of Rhodes, and fashioned the hanging gardens of Babylon. It is obvious that groups outperform individuals, especially when performance requires multiple skills, judgments, and experiences. Many educators, however, overlook opportunities to use groups to enhance student learning and increase their own success.

Assessment requires groups. But not just any group. There are ineffective as well as effective groups and, therefore, teachers have to know how to structure groups to maximize their productivity. To structure groups so that they are effective, educators have to know the following:

1. The nature of the cooperative learning (what is and is not a cooperative group, the nature of cooperative learning)

2. The teacher's role in using cooperative learning

3. The five basic elements that make cooperation work

4. The benefits of using cooperative learning for instruction and assessment

Not All Groups Are Effective

There is nothing magical about working in a group. Some kinds of learning groups facilitate student learning, enhance assessment, and increase the quality of life in the classroom. Other types of learning groups hinder student learning, interfere with assessment, and create disharmony and dissatisfaction with classroom life. To use groups effectively for learning and assessment, you must know what is and is not a cooperative group. Generally, groups may be classified into four categories (Johnson & F. Johnson, 2003):

1. Pseudo-Learning Group: Students are assigned to work together, but they have no interest in doing so. They believe they will be evaluated by being ranked from the highest performer to the lowest performer. While on the surface, students talk to each other, under the surface, they are competing. They see each other as rivals who must be defeated, block or interfere with each other's learning, hide information from each other, attempt to mislead and confuse each other, and distrust each other. The result is that the sum of the whole is less than the potential of the individual members. Students would achieve more if they were working alone.

2. Traditional Classroom Learning Group: Students are assigned to work together and accept that they have to do so. Assignments are structured, however, so that very little joint work is required. Students believe that they will be evaluated and rewarded as individuals, not as members of the group. They interact primarily to clarify how assignments are to be done. They seek each other's information but have no motivation to teach what they know to their groupmates. Helping and sharing is minimized. Some students loaf, seeking a free ride on the efforts of their more conscientious groupmates. The conscientious members feel exploited and do less. The result is that the sum of the whole is more than the potential of some of the members, but the more hard-working and conscientious students would perform at a higher level if they worked alone.

3. Cooperative Learning Group: Students are assigned to work together, and they are happy to do so. They believe that their success depends on the efforts of all group members. There are five defining characteristics. First, the group goal of maximizing all members' learning provides a compelling common purpose that motivates members to roll up their sleeves and accomplish something beyond their individual achievements. Members believe that "they sink or swim together," and "if one of us fails, we all fail." Second, group members hold themselves and each other accountable for doing high-quality work to achieve their mutual goals. Third, group members work face-to-face to produce joint work products. They do real work together. Students promote each other's success through helping, sharing, assisting, explaining, and encouraging. They provide both academic and personal support based on a commitment to and caring about each other. Fourth, group members are taught social skills and are expected to use them to coordinate their efforts and achieve their goals. Both taskwork and teamwork skills are emphasized. All members accept the responsibility for providing leadership. Last, groups analyze how effectively they are achieving their goals and how well members are working together. There is an emphasis on continuous improvement of the quality of learning and teamwork processes. The result is that the group is more than a sum of its parts, and all students perform at a higher level academically than they would if they worked alone.

4. High-Performance Cooperative Learning Group: This is a group that meets all the criteria for being a cooperative learning group and outperforms all reasonable expectations, given its membership. What differentiates the high-performance group from the cooperative learning group is the level of commitment members have to each other and the group's success. The bad news about high-performance cooperative groups is that they are rare. Most groups never achieve this level of development. All a teacher can do is create cooperative learning groups and hope that some excel beyond all expectations.

To use learning groups effectively for instruction and for assessment, you must realize that not all groups are cooperative groups. Placing people in the same room and calling them a cooperative group does not make them one. Study groups, project groups, lab groups, home rooms, and reading groups are groups, but they are not necessarily cooperative. The teacher's responsibility is to assign students to learning groups, monitor their work, diagnose where on the group performance curve the groups are, strengthen the basic elements of cooperation, and move groups up the performance curve until they are truly cooperative learning groups.

Implementing Cooperative Learning Groups

Cooperative learning groups exist when students work together to accomplish shared goals. Students perceive that they can reach their learning goals if, and only if, the other students in the learning group also reach their goals (Deutsch, 1962; Johnson & Johnson, 1989). Thus students seek outcomes that are beneficial to all those with whom they are cooperatively linked. Students are given two responsibilities: to complete the assignment and to ensure that all other group members complete the assignment. A criteria-referenced evaluation system is used. Any assignment in any curriculum for any age student can be done cooperatively.

There are three types of cooperative learning groups. **Formal cooperative learning groups** consist of students working together, for one class period to several weeks, to achieve shared learning goals and jointly complete specific tasks and assignments (Johnson, Johnson, & Holubec, 1998b). In formal cooperative learning groups, teachers make a set of preinstructional decisions, explain the task and the positive interdependence, monitor students' learning and intervene within the groups to provide task assistance or to increase students' interpersonal and group skills, and assess students' learning and helping students process how well their groups functioned.

Informal cooperative learning groups consist of having students work together to achieve a joint learning goal in temporary, ad hoc groups that last from a few minutes to one class period (Johnson, Johnson, & Holubec, 1998a). During a lecture, demonstration, or film, informal cooperative learning can be used to focus student attention on the material to be learned, set a mood conducive to learning, help set expectations as to what will be covered in a class session, ensure that students cognitively process and rehearse the material being taught, summarize what was learned and precue the next session, and provide closure to an instructional session. The procedure for using informal cooperative learning during a lecture entails having three-to-five-minute **focused discussions** before and after the lecture (i.e., bookends) and two-to-three-minute interspersing **pair discussions** throughout the lecture.

Cooperative base groups are long-term, heterogeneous cooperative learning groups with stable membership whose primary responsibilities are to provide support, encouragement, and assistance to make academic progress and develop cognitively and socially in healthy ways as well as holding each other accountable for striving to learn (Johnson, Johnson, & Holubec, 1998a). Typically, cooperative base groups (1) are heterogeneous in membership, (2) meet regularly (for example, daily or biweekly), and (3) last for the duration of the semester, year, or until all members have graduated. When students know that the base group will stay together for some time, they become committed to find ways to motivate and encourage their groupmates and solve any problems in working together. The procedure for using base groups is to assign students to base groups of three to four members, have them meet at the beginning and end of each class session (or week) to complete academic tasks, such as checking each members' homework, routine tasks, such as taking attendance, and personal support tasks, such as listening sympathetically to personal problems or providing guidance for writing a paper.

The Teacher's Role in Formal Cooperative Learning

Preinstructional Decisions

Specifying the Instructional Objectives

To plan for a lesson, you must know what the lesson is aimed at accomplishing. You need to specify academic objectives (based on a conceptual or a task analysis) and social-skills objectives that detail what interpersonal and small-group skills you wish to emphasize during the lesson.

Deciding on the Size of the Group

To assign students to groups, you must decide (1) how large the groups should be, (2) how students should be assigned to a group, (3) how long the groups will exist, and (4) what combination of groups will be used in the lesson. While cooperative learning groups typically range in size from two to four, the basic rule of thumb is: The smaller the better. There is, however, no ideal size for a cooperative learning group.

Assigning Students to Groups

There are a number of ways to assign students to groups (see Johnson, Johnson, & Holubec, 1994, 1998b). Perhaps the easiest and most effective way is to assign students to groups randomly. A teacher can divide the number of students in the class by the size of the group desired (e.g., thirty students divided by group size three equals counting off by ten). A related procedure is stratified random assignment where, for example, a pretest is given, the class is divided into high, medium, and low scorers, and one student from each category is randomly assigned to a triad. A third method is the formation of teacher-selected groups, and a fourth method is creating support groups for each isolated student. The teacher asks students to list three classmates with whom they would like to work. From their lists, isolates who no one wants to work with may be identified. The teacher then builds a group of skillful and supportive students around each isolated student. The least-recommended procedure is to have students select their own groups.

Group Size Depends On "TEAM"
T = Time Limits
E = Students' Experience in Working in Groups
A = Students' Age
M = Materials and Equipment Available

Arranging the Room

Members of a learning group should sit close enough to each other that they can share materials, maintain eye contact with all group members, talk to each other quietly without disrupting the other learning groups, and exchange ideas and materials in a comfortable atmosphere. The groups need to be far enough apart so that they do not interfere with each other's learning. Last, the groups should be arranged so that the teacher has a clear access lane to every group.

Planning the Instructional Materials

The types of task students are required to complete determine what materials are needed for the lesson. You, the teacher, decide how materials are to be arranged and distributed among group members to maximize their participation and achievement. Usually, you will wish to distribute materials to communicate that the assignment is to be a joint (not an individual) effort by creating **materials interdependence** (giving each group only one copy of the materials so students will have to work together to be successful), **information interdependence** (arranging materials like a jigsaw puzzle so that each student has part of the materials needed to complete the assignment so every member participates for the group to be successful), and **interdependence from outside competition** by structuring materials into an intergroup tournament format and having groups compete to see who has learned the most.

Assigning Roles to Ensure Interdependence

In planning the lesson, teachers think through what actions need to occur for student learning to be maximized. Teachers can then define those actions as roles and assign a role to each group member. Examples of roles include **summarizer** (who restates the group's major conclusions or answers) and **checker of understanding** (who ensures that all group members can explain how to arrive at an answer or conclusion). Assigning complementary and interconnected roles to group members is an effective method of teaching students social skills and fostering positive interdependence.

Structuring Task and Positive Interdependence

Explaining the Academic Task

The teacher informs students what the assignment is, what students have to do to complete the assignment, and how to do it.

Explaining Criteria for Success

Cooperative learning requires criterion-based evaluation—that is, a fixed set of standards for judging the achievement of each student. Sometimes, improvement (doing better this week than last week) may be set as the criterion of excellence. To promote intergroup cooperation, you may also set criteria for the whole class to reach: "If we as a class can score over 520 words correct on our vocabulary test, each student will receive two bonus points."

Structuring Positive Interdependence

To ensure that students think "**We, not me,**" teachers say to students, "You have three responsibilities: You are responsible for learning the assigned material, you are responsible for all members of your group learning the assigned material, and you are responsible for all class members learning the assigned material." Positive interdependence is the heart of cooperative learning. Without positive interdependence, cooperation does not exist. Students must believe that they are in a sink-or-swim-together learning situation. Teachers create positive interdependence (see Johnson & Johnson, 1992a, 1992b) by structuring joint learning goals (**positive goal interdependence**) and supplementing it with other types of positive interdependence (such as reward, role, resource, or identity).

Structuring Individual Accountability

In cooperative groups, everyone has to do his or her fair share of the work. An underlying purpose of cooperative learning is to make each group member a stronger individual in his or her own right. This is accomplished by holding all members accountable to learn the assigned material and help other group members learn. This is done by assessing the performance of each individual member and giving the results back to the individual and the group to compare to preset criteria.

Structuring Intergroup Cooperation

You can extend the positive outcomes resulting from cooperative learning throughout a whole class by structuring intergroup cooperation. You establish class goals as well as group and individual goals.

Specifying Desired Behaviors

When you use cooperative learning, you must teach students the small-group and interpersonal skills they need to work effectively with each other. In cooperative learning groups, students must learn both academic subject matter (**taskwork**) and the interpersonal and small-group skills required to work as part of a group (**teamwork**). If students do not learn the teamwork skills, then they cannot complete the taskwork. The greater the members' teamwork skills, the higher will be the quality and quantity of their learning.

Monitoring and Intervening

A teacher's responsibilities begin in earnest when the cooperative learning groups start working. Teachers observe the interaction among group members to assess students' (1) academic progress and (2) appropriate use of interpersonal and small-group skills. Observations can be formal (with an observation schedule on which frequencies are tallied) or anecdotal (informal descriptions of students' statements and actions). Based on their observations, teachers can then intervene to improve students' academic learning or interpersonal and small-group skills (or both).

In intervening in groups, the teacher may clarify instructions, review important procedures and strategies for completing the assignment, answer questions, and teach task skills as necessary. One way to intervene is to interview a cooperative learning group by asking them (1) "What are you doing?" (2) "Why are you doing it?" and (3) "How will it help you?" In addition, there may be students who do not have the necessary social skills to be effective and positive group members. In these cases, you will wish to intervene to suggest more effective procedures for working together and specific social skills to use.

Assessing Learning and Processing Interaction

Providing Closure to the Lesson

Informal cooperative learning procedures often are used to provide closure to lessons by having students summarize the major points in the lesson, recall ideas, and identify final questions for the teacher. At the end of the lesson, students should be able to summarize what they have learned and to understand how they will use it in future lessons.

Assessing the Quality and Quantity of Learning

Tests should be given, and papers and presentations should be graded. The learning of group members must be assessed by a criterion-referenced system for cooperative learning to be successful.

Processing How Well the Group Functioned

Group processing occurs at two levels—in each learning group and in the class as a whole. When students have completed the assignment, they should have time to describe what member actions were helpful (and unhelpful) in completing the group's work and make decisions about what behaviors to continue or change. In a whole-class discussion, teachers give the class feedback based on their observations and have students share incidents that occurred in their groups.

Five Basic Elements

There is an old story about twelve men in a lifeboat. One of the men announced that he had decided to bore a series of holes in the bottom of the boat. "You can't do that," the other eleven men cried. "Why not?" the man answered. "I've divided the boat into twelve equal parts. Each of us has part of the boat. We can do anything to our part of the boat we want to. I've decided to drill holes in the bottom of my part. You do anything you want with your part. It's your right!" Many people see the world in these terms. They are unaware of their interdependence with others and the ways that their actions spread out like ripples in a pond to touch others.

To structure lessons and instructional units so students do in fact work cooperatively with each other, you must understand the basic elements that make cooperation work. Mastering the basic elements of cooperation allows you to

1. Take your existing instructional units, curricula, and courses and structure them cooperatively

2. Tailor cooperative learning instructional units to your unique instructional needs, circumstances, curricula, subject areas, students, and assessment goals

3. Diagnose the problems some students may have in working together and intervene to increase the effectiveness of the student learning groups

4. Ensure that high-quality assessments at both the group and individual levels take place

For cooperation to work well, you must structure five essential elements in each lesson (Johnson & Johnson, 1989). **The first and most important element is positive interdependence** (i.e., the perception that you are linked with others in a way so that you cannot succeed unless they do [and vice versa]; that is, their work benefits you, and your work benefits them). Students must believe that they sink or swim together. In every lesson, mutual goals need to be structured so students are clear they are responsible not only for their own learning but for the learning of their groupmates also. In addition, positive interdependence may be strengthened through joint rewards, complementary resources, complementary roles, a division of labor, and a joint identity, all of which create interdependence. Strong positive interdependence creates a setting in which valid and reliable assessments can take place.

The second essential element of cooperative learning is individual and group accountability. The group must be accountable for achieving its goals. **Group accountability** exists when the overall performance of the group is assessed and the results are given back to all group members to compare against a standard of performance. Each member must be accountable for contributing his or her share of the work (which ensures that no one can hitchhike on the work of others). **Individual accountability** exists when the performance of each individual member is assessed, the results given back to the individual and the group to compare against a standard of performance, and each member is held responsible by groupmates for contributing his or her fair share to the group's success. The purpose of cooperative learning groups is to make each member a stronger individual in his or her right. Students learn together so that they can subsequently perform higher as individuals. The group has to be clear about its goals and be able to measure (1) its progress in achieving them and (2) the individual efforts of each of its members.

The third essential component of cooperative learning is promotive interaction, preferably face-to-face. Promotive interaction occurs when members share resources and help, support, and encourage each other's efforts to learn. Cooperative learning groups are both an academic support system (every student has someone who is committed to helping him or her learn) and a personal support system (every student has someone who is committed to him or her as a person). In addition, there are important cognitive activities and interpersonal dynamics that can only occur when students promote each other's learning. This includes orally explaining how to solve problems, discussing the nature of the concepts being learned, teaching one's knowledge to classmates, and connecting present with past learning. It is through promoting each other's learning face-to-face that members become personally committed to each other as well as to their mutual goals.

The fourth essential element of cooperative learning is teaching students the required interpersonal and small-group skills. In cooperative learning groups, students are required to learn academic subject matter (taskwork) and also to learn the interpersonal and small-group skills required to function as part of a group (teamwork). Cooperative learning is inherently more complex than competitive or solitary learning because students have to engage simultaneously in taskwork and teamwork. Group members must know how to provide effective leadership, decision making, trust building, communication, and conflict-management and be motivated to use the prerequisite skills. Teamwork skills have to be taught just as purposefully and precisely as do academic skills (Johnson, 1991, 2003; Johnson & F. Johnson, 2003). Social skills may be assessed by (1) assigning each group member a role (skill), (2) observing the frequency and quality with which the role is performed, and (3) giving points when the role performance is up to the preset criterion.

The fifth essential component of cooperative learning is group processing. Group processing exists when group members discuss how well they are achieving their goals and maintaining effective working relationships. Groups need to describe what member actions are helpful and unhelpful and make decisions about what behaviors to continue or change. Continuous improvement of the process of learning results from the careful analysis of how members are working together and determining how group effectiveness can be enhanced.

Power of Cooperation

Since 1897, over 550 experimental and 100 correlational studies have been conducted on cooperative, competitive, and individualistic efforts (see Johnson & Johnson, 1989) by a wide variety of researchers in different decades with different age subjects, in different subject areas, and in different settings. Research participants have varied as to economic class, age, sex, nationality, and cultural background. A wide variety of research tasks, ways of structuring cooperation, and measures of the

Table 2.1   Mean Effect Sizes of Social Interdependence Studies

Dependent Variable	Cooperative Vs. Competitive	Cooperative Vs. Individualistic	Competitive Vs. Individualistic
Achievement	0.67	0.64	0.30
Interpersonal Attraction	0.67	0.60	0.08
Social Support	0.62	0.70	−0.13
Self-Esteem	0.58	0.44	−0.23

SOURCE: Johnson, D. W., & Johnson, R., (1989). *Cooperation and competition: Theory and research.* Edina, MN: Interaction Book Company.

dependent variables have been used. Many different researchers have conducted the research with markedly different orientations working in different settings, countries, and decades. The research on cooperation has validity and generalizability rarely found in educational literature. The research has focused on numerous outcomes, which may be subsumed within the broad and interrelated categories of effort to achieve, quality of relationships, psychological health, and social skills (Johnson & Johnson, 1989). See Table 2.1 and Figure 2.1.

Effort to Achieve

From Table 2.1, it may be seen that cooperation promotes considerably greater effort to achieve than do competitive or individual efforts. Effort exerted to achieve includes such variables as achievement and productivity, long-term retention, on-task behavior, use of higher-level reasoning strategies, generation of new ideas and solutions, transfer of what is learned within one situation to another, intrinsic motivation, achievement motivation, continuing motivation to learn, and positive attitudes toward learning and school. Overall, cooperation tends to promote higher achievement than competitive or individual efforts (effect-sizes = 0.67 and 0.64, respectively). The impact of cooperative learning on achievement means that if schools wish to prepare students to take proficiency tests to meet local and state standards, the use of cooperative learning should dominate instructional practice.

An important aspect of school life is engagement in learning. One indication of engagement in learning is time on task. Cooperators spent considerably more time on task than did competitors (effect size = 0.76) or students working alone (effect size = 1.17). In addition, students working cooperatively tended to (1) be more involved in activities and tasks, (2) attach greater importance to success, and (3) engage in more

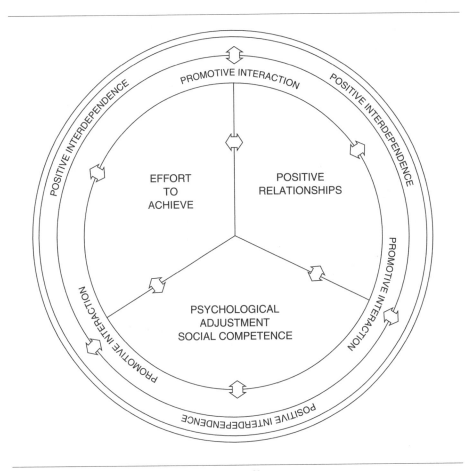

Figure 2.1   Outcomes of Cooperative Efforts

SOURCE: Johnson, D. W., & Johnson, R., (1989). *Cooperation and competition: Theory and research.* Edina, MN: Interaction Book Company.

on-task behavior and less apathetic, off-task, disruptive behaviors. Last, cooperative experiences, compared with competitive and individualistic ones, have been found to promote more positive attitudes toward the task and the experience of working on it (effect-sizes = 0.57 and 0.42, respectively).

Quality of Relationships

Quality of relationships includes such variables as interpersonal attraction, liking, cohesion, esprit de corps, and social support. The degree of emotional bonding that exists among students has a profound effect on students' social and emotional learning. The more positive the relationships among students and between students and faculty, the lower the absenteeism and dropout rates and the greater the commitment to group goals, feelings of personal responsibility to the group, willingness to take on difficult tasks, motivation and persistence in working toward goal achievement, satisfaction and morale, willingness to endure pain and frustration on behalf of the group, willingness to defend the group against external criticism or attack, willingness to listen to and be influenced by colleagues, commitment to each other's professional growth and success, and productivity (Johnson & F. Johnson, 2003).

There have been over 175 studies that have investigated the relative impact of cooperative, competitive, and individualistic efforts on quality of relationships and another 106 studies on social support (Johnson & Johnson, 1989). From Table 2.1, it may be seen that cooperation generally promoted greater interpersonal attraction among individuals than did competitive or individual efforts (effect sizes = 0.66 and 0.60 respectively). Cooperative experiences tended to promote greater social support than did competitive (effect-size = 0.62) or individual (effect-size = 0.70) efforts. Stronger effects were found for peer support than for superior (teacher) support. The high-quality studies tended to have even more powerful effects.

Psychological Health

Ashley Montagu (1966) was fond of saying, "With few exceptions, the solitary animal is, in any species, an abnormal creature." Karen Horney (1937) said, "The neurotic individual is someone who is inappropriately competitive and, therefore, unable to cooperate with others." Montagu and Horney recognized that the essence of psychological health is the ability to develop and maintain cooperative relationships. More specifically, **psychological health** is the ability (cognitive capacities, motivational orientations, and social skills) to build, maintain, and appropriately modify interdependent relationships with others to succeed in achieving goals (Johnson & Johnson, 1989). People who are unable to do so often (1) become depressed, anxious, frustrated, and lonely, (2) tend to feel afraid, inadequate, helpless, hopeless, and isolated, and (3) rigidly cling to unproductive and ineffective ways of coping with adversity. With our students and colleagues, we have conducted a series of studies relating cooperative, competitive, and individualistic efforts and attitudes to various indices of psychological health. The samples studied included middle-class junior high students, middle-class high school seniors, high-school-aged juvenile prisoners, adult prisoners, Olympic ice-hockey players, and adult stepcouples. The diversity of the samples studied and the variety of measures of psychological health provide considerable generalizability of the results of the studies. A strong relationship was found between cooperativeness and psychological health, a mixed picture was found with competitiveness and psychological health, and a strong relationship was found between an individualistic orientation and psychological pathology.

Use of Criterion-Referenced Rather Than Norm-Referenced Procedures

Closely related to the issue of cooperative versus competitive contexts for learning is the issue of criterion-referenced versus norm-referenced assessment procedures. Norm-referenced assessment and evaluation procedures are inherently competitive as student performances are compared with one another to determine the quality and quantity of students' work. Student performances can be placed in a normal curve, and grades are determined by fixed percentages in each grade category (10 percent A's, 20 percent B's, 40 percent C's, 20 percent D's, and 10 percent F's). Alternatively, student performances can just be ranked from highest to lowest. While norm-referenced procedures are often assumed to be commonly used, a national survey conducted by Astin (1993) on college and university teaching indicated that only about 22 percent of all faculty graded on the curve.

An underlying foundational requirement for successful use of learning groups is criterion-referenced assessment. Criterion-referenced procedures assess the quality or quantity of student performances on an absolute grading scale. In a criterion-referenced scheme, absolute criteria are set (90 percent for an A), and anyone and everyone who meets or exceeds this criterion receives that grade. It is possible for everyone (or no one) to get an A. Criterion-referenced procedures are essential when groups are required to produce a group product. It is counterproductive to ask students to work together on projects (and perhaps share a grade) and then pit them against one another by grading them on the curve at the end of the course. One of the most common reasons that groupwork fails is that faculty require students to work cooperatively while a norm-referenced grading is used in the course.

Summary and Conclusions

There is nothing magical about working in a group. Some kinds of learning groups facilitate student learning, enhance assessment, and increase the quality of life in the classroom while other types of learning groups hinder student learning, interfere with assessment, and create disharmony and dissatisfaction with classroom life. To use groups effectively for learning and assessment, you must know what is and is not a cooperative group and be able to change pseudo and traditional learning groups to cooperative learning groups. Cooperative learning groups exist when students work together to accomplish shared goals. Any assignment in any subject area may be structured cooperatively. There are three types of cooperative learning groups: Formal cooperative learning groups, informal cooperative learning groups, and cooperative base groups. In formal cooperative learning groups, teachers make a set of preinstructional decisions, explain the task and the positive interdependence, monitor students' learning and intervene within the groups to provide task assistance or to increase students' interpersonal and group skills, assess students' learning, and help students process how well their groups functioned. The procedure for using informal cooperative learning entails having three-to-five-minute focused discussions before and after the lecture (i.e., bookends) and two-to-three-minute interspersing pair discussions throughout the lecture. The procedure for using base groups is to have the groups meet at the beginning and end of each class session (or week) to complete academic tasks, such as checking each members' homework, routine tasks, such as taking attendance, and personal support tasks, such as listening sympathetically to personal problems or providing guidance for writing a paper. To use groups for assessment purposes, the groups have to be structured cooperatively.

CHAPTER 3

Developing an Assessment Plan for Groups

P hotographer Louis Faurer, who took magnificent black and white photographs of everyday people doing things so ordinary that we tend to overlook them, attributed much of his success to his relationship with noted Swiss-American photographer, Robert Frank. Faurer used reflections, double exposures, and sandwiched negatives to convey the complexity in city life. The tension between physical intimacy and psychological distance is a constant in his work. Faurer worked very closely with (and was greatly influenced by) Frank. In writing about the friendship and partnership between them, Faurer stated, "We influenced each other without jealousy and without resentment . . . We influenced each other without any tension, with total acceptance" (display caption to Faurer exhibit, The Art Institute of Chicago).

To capitalize on the power of groups for assessment, teachers must make assessment plans and make decisions about a number of assessment issues.

Assessment Issues

To plan, conduct, and manage meaningful assessments, you need to answer the following questions (Johnson & Johnson, 1996, 2002):

1. Will individual, group, or both levels of assessments be made?

2. What are the processes and outcomes that will be assessed?

3. What is the sequence of instructional tasks?

4. What are the assessment procedures that may be used?

5. What is the purpose of the assessment?

6. In what setting will the assessment be conducted?

7. Who are the stakeholders in the assessment?

8. What assessment procedure should be used?

Levels of Assessment

Assessment plans focus on two levels: group and individual. Either or both may be included in the plan. At the individual level, students may (1) engage in self-assessment, (2) engage in peer assessment, and (3) be assessed individually by the teacher. Individual assessments are needed in every aspect of education. At the group level, the teacher assesses the performance of the group as a whole. Examples of situations in which group assessments are needed are group projects, group experiments in subjects such as chemistry and physics, group videos in literature and social studies classes, plays in drama classes, team sports in physical education, and so many others that they cannot all be listed here. Groups provide an important use of assessment plans, and therefore, educators need to understand how to make assessment plans for groups. See Figure 3.1, which illustrates the process of assessment.

Outcomes Assessed

There is an old saying, What gets measured gets done. What teachers assess may be the single most powerful message as to what teachers value and wish to accomplish. Some of the most common targets of assessment are (Johnson & Johnson, 1996, 2002)

1. **Academic Learning**: What students know, understand, and retain over time. This includes declarative, procedural, schematic, and strategic knowledge acquired in a domain (e.g., American History).

2. **Reasoning**: The quality of students' reasoning, conceptual frameworks, use of the scientific method and problem solving, and construction of academic arguments. This includes broad abilities that consist of particular complexes of cognitive

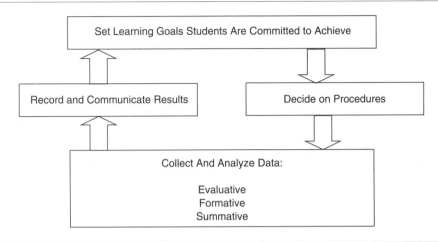

Figure 3.1   Process of Assessment

processes (such as thinking) that underlie the verbal, quantitative, and spatial reasoning—as well as comprehension, problem solving, and decision making skills within domains and more generally across domains.

3. **Skills And Competencies**: Oral and written communication skills, teamwork skills, research skills, skills of organizing and analyzing information, technology skills, skills of coping with stress and adversity, conflict resolution skills. Personal, social, and civic competencies need to be assessed as well as cognitive ones.

4. **Attitudes**: The attitudes students develop, such as a love of learning, commitment to being a responsible citizen, desire to read, liking scientific reasoning, self-respect, liking of diversity, commitment to making the world a better place, and many others.

5. **Work Habits**: The work habits students develop, such as completing work on time, using time wisely, meeting responsibilities, striving for quality work, continuously improving one's work, striving to add value to each job one does, and so forth.

The checklist, "Your Assessment Plan," gives a quick overview of assessment goals and methods and can be useful for mapping out your own class assessment approaches.

Your Assessment Plan

Given below are generic assessment targets and procedures. In planning your assessment program, check the targets that you wish to assess and then check the procedures you wish to use. Match the procedures with the targets so it is clear how you will assess each target.

What Is Assessed	Procedures Used to Assess
_____ Academic learning	_____ Goal-setting conferences
_____ Reasoning process, strategies	_____ Standardized tests
_____ Skills and competencies	_____ Teacher-made tests
_____ Attitudes	_____ Written compositions
_____ Work habits	_____ Oral presentations
	_____ Projects
	_____ Portfolios
	_____ Observations
	_____ Questionnaires
	_____ Interviews
	_____ Learning logs and journals
	_____ Student management teams

Sequence of Instructional Tasks

In making an assessment plan, teachers need to sequence instructional tasks so that diagnostic, formative, and summative assessments are possible.

Assessment Procedures

After deciding which student achievements to assess, you need to decide which procedures you will use to determine the extent to which students are achieving the intended learning outcomes of instruction. The procedures you can use include the following:

Goal-setting conferences	Simulations
Standardized tests	Questionnaires
Teacher-made tests, quizzes, exams	Interviews
Written compositions	Learning logs and journals
Oral presentations	Student management teams
Projects, experiments	Total-quality learning procedures
Portfolios	Teacher assessment teams
Observations	Student-led parent conferences
Record keeping (attendance, participation homework, extra credit)	

SOURCE: Johnson & Johnson, 1996, 2002

Purpose of Assessment

The purposes for assessing may be to (1) diagnose students' present level of knowledge and skills, (2) monitor progress toward learning goals to help form the instructional program, and (3) provide data to judge the final level of students' learning.

1. **Diagnostic assessments** are conducted at the beginning of an instructional unit or course to determine the present level of students' knowledge, skills, interests, and attitudes. This enables teachers to set realistic but challenging learning goals and plan appropriate instructional experiences.

2. **Formative assessments** are conducted periodically throughout the instructional unit or course to monitor progress and provide feedback concerning advancement toward learning goals. Its intention is to facilitate or form learning.

3. **Summative assessments** are conducted at the end of an instructional unit or semester to judge the final quality and quantity of student achievement, the success of the instructional program, or both. They sum up performance and provide the data for giving grades and determining the extent to which goals and objectives have been met and desired outcomes achieved. The judgments about student achievement are then communicated to interested audiences.

Diagnostic, formative, and summative assessments may take place to improve the process of learning or to determine the outcomes of learning. In conducting formative assessments, the focus may be on both the process of learning and the outcomes of learning. In conducting summative assessments, the focus is primarily on outcomes.

Setting of Assessments

Assessments may take place in artificial situations (such as the classroom) or in authentic or real-life settings. **Authentic assessment** requires students to demonstrate desired skills or procedures in real-life contexts. Group assessments are typically easier to conduct in an authentic assessment.

Stakes and Stakeholders

There are at least four audiences for the results of assessments of students' learning, instructional programs, and the effectiveness of a school: students and their parents, teachers, administrators, and policy makers. For each of these audiences, assessments can be of high or low importance. In designing and conducting assessments, you must determine who the audiences for the assessment will be and what kind of stake they have in its results. The danger of low-stake assessments is that students and faculty may not take them seriously. The danger of high-stake assessments is that students and faculty may be tempted to cheat in some manner.

Methods of Assessment

Periodically, after summative assessments have been made, teachers assign value to students' work. Teachers can symbolize the value with smiley faces, written comments, or grades. In deciding how to assign value, teachers must choose whether to make judgments based on a criterion-referenced or a norm-referenced procedure. The **criterion-referenced procedure** assigns a value or grade to a score according to a predetermined standard. Criterion-referenced evaluation is used in cooperative and individual learning. The **norm-referenced procedure** assigns a value or grade to a score based on a comparison to other scores. Norm-referenced evaluation is used as part of competitive learning.

Criteria-Referenced Evaluation

Criterion-referenced or categorical judgments are made by adopting a fixed set of standards and judging the achievement of each student against these standards. Every student who can achieve up to the standard passes, and every student who cannot, fails. If the criterion is for students to demonstrate ability to use propositional logic in solving a series of chemistry problems, then a teacher takes each student's answers and judges whether or not they have done so. A

Table 3.1   Criterion-Referenced Grading Sample

Grade	Percent Correct
A	95 – 100
B	85 – 94
C	75 – 84
D	65 – 74
F	Less than 64

common version of criterion-referenced evaluation involves assigning letter grades on the basis of the percentage of test items answered correctly. An example is shown in Table 3.1.

Criterion-referenced evaluation was first recommended as part of mastery or competency-based instruction in the 1920s and was widely used in the 1930s. Yet in the 1940s and 1950s, its use declined. In the 1960s, however, a revival of interest in criterion-referenced evaluation resulted from the increased emphasis on behavioral objectives, the sequencing and individualizing of instruction, mastery learning, and cooperative learning. If teachers can state their instructional objectives in measurable terms, then the teacher can determine whether a student has achieved the objectives.

Norm-Referenced Evaluation

Norm-referenced evaluation uses the achievement of other students as a frame of reference for judging the performance of an individual. The general procedure is to administer a test to a large sample of people like those for whom the measure is designed. This group, known as the *norm group,* provides a distribution of scores against which the score of any single person can be compared. Classroom teachers usually use norm-referenced evaluation procedures by **grading on a curve**. Grading on a curve was one of many proposals for educational reform in the 1930s; it represented an attempt to adopt in the classroom the same procedures used by publishers of standardized tests. To grade on a curve, teachers define the norm group as all the students in the class for which the grades are to be assigned and assume that the distribution of test scores follows the form known as the normal curve (see Figure 3.2).

The way in which the norm group is selected is crucial to the fairness and validity of the judgments made. Although there are statistical advantages to assuming that assessment results are normally distributed, (1) teacher-made assessment measures are rarely designed to

Table 3.2   Norm-Referenced Grading

Grading on the Curve	Characteristics
15 percent receive A's	Compares student performances to each other
20 percent receive B's	Creates competition among students
30 percent receive C's	Assumes that distribution of test scores is a normal curve
20 percent receive D's	Teacher-made tests are not designed to give normal distributions
15 percent receive F's	Class sizes are typically too small to expect a normal distribution

give normal distributions, and (2) class sizes are typically too small to expect a normal distribution. It takes several hundred scores to potentially have a normal distribution. Terwilliger (1971) concludes that these defects are so serious and so common that it is impossible to justify the practice of grading on a curve.

There are numerous disadvantages to using norm-referenced evaluation procedures (Johnson & Johnson, 1999). Norm-referenced evaluation tends to

1. Increase student anxiety, which interferes with learning complex tasks and new information. High anxiety especially interferes with adaptive problem-solving.

2. Motivate individuals to exert minimal effort. In competitions, chronic winners exert only enough effort to win, and chronic losers exert little or no effort at all.

3. Create extrinsic motivation. Winning tends to become more important than learning.

4. Reduce intrinsic motivation to learn for interest in or enjoyment of an activity for its own sake.

5. Increase the frequency with which students cheat. Students tend to become more committed to winning at any cost.

6. Create a situation in which students may internalize the values of bettering others and taking joy in others' mistakes. Students tend to become less committed to values of fairness and justice and more self-oriented.

7. Promote contingent self-acceptance, in which the value of self and others is contingent on winning.

8. Result in overgeneralization of results to all aspects of a person's being. Winning in one arena tends to result in a feeling a superiority in all arenas. Losing in one arena tends to result in a feeling of inferiority in all arenas.

9. Create anger, hostility, and dislike toward those who win. Losing tends to promote depression and aggression toward winners and judges.

10. Promote a view of life as a dog-eat-dog struggle in which only the strongest survive.

Total-Quality Learning

Traditionally, it is the outcomes of instruction that have been the focus of assessment. W. Edwards Deming (Deming & Epley, 2000) and other advocates of total-quality management in business and industry, however, stress that instead of measuring outcomes, the emphasis should be on improving the process by which instructional assessment and learning take place. Continuous improvement of the processes of instruction and learning can only take place if assessment is continuous. The continuous improvement of instruction and learning consists of seven steps (Johnson & Johnson, 1994):

1. **Form teams**. To promote total quality in a school, both students and teachers have to be assigned to teams (to cooperative learning groups and collegial teaching teams, respectively). The teams are charged with maintaining the quality of the work of its members.

2. **Select a process for improvement**. The team needs a specific, definable process to work on. The process needs to be significant, and it must be in the power of the team to change the process. Students, therefore, focus on the process they are using to learn.

3. **Define the process**. Students define their learning process by drawing a picture of it. Two common ways to picture a process are the flow chart and the cause-and-effect diagram.

4. **Engage in the process**. Team members engage in the process and measure each of its steps.

5. **Gather information** about the process, display the data, and analyze it. There are three parts to this step:

a. The team identifies quantifiable factors (such as time). If a factor cannot bemeasured, it cannot be improved (conversely, to be able to improve it, you must be able to measure it).
b. The team develops a design for gathering the relevant data. This includes specifying what data will be collected, who will collect it, when it will be collected, and how it will be collected. A check sheet or observation form is a common way to gather data.
c. The team analyzes and portrays the data in ways that help members understand it easily. Common ways to portray data are the Pareto chart, run chart, scatter diagram, and histogram.

6. **Creating and implementing an improvement plan.** A plan is created on how the process is to be modified to improve its effectiveness. The team then implements the plan. The focus is on making small, incremental improvements in a process day after day after day. The team carefully evaluates the implementation (members gather more data). If the modified process works, the team adopts it. If it does not work, the team redesigns it and tries it out again on a small basis.

7. **Institutionalizing changes that work.** Team members ensure that there is no backsliding (reverting to the old practices) by taking new data samples forever, analyzing them, revising the plan, and revising the process.

Deming and Epley (2000) believe that if teachers concentrate on this continuous improvement of learning and instruction, the quality of students' learning will take care of itself.

Summary

In making an assessment plan that is then implemented and carried out to fruition, there are at least eight issues that have to be addressed. Teachers may assess individuals, groups, or both. The specific processes and outcomes that will be assessed need to be determined; the potential outcomes include knowledge, reasoning processes, skills and competencies, attitudes and values, and work habits. The sequence of instructional tasks that students will complete is then determined. The assessment procedures are then formulated; procedures include tests, observations, portfolios, reports, and so forth. The purpose of assessments may be diagnostic, formative, or summative. The setting in which assessments take place may be artificial or authentic. The stakeholders include students, parents, teachers,

My Assessment Plan

1. What are the purposes of the assessment?
   a. _____
   b. _____
   c. _____
   d. _____

2. What is the focus of the assessment?
   _____ Process of learning   _____ Outcomes of learning
   _____ Process of instruction   _____ Outcomes of instruction

3. In what setting will the assessment take place?

4. The assessment will be aimed at
   _____ Academic learning   _____ Attitudes
   _____ Level of reasoning, critical _____ Work habits
   thinking
   _____ Skills and competencies

5. The assessment procedures used will be
   _____ Standardized tests   _____ Portfolios
   _____ Teacher-made tests   _____ Observation

(Continued)

(Continued)

_____ Compositions	_____ Interviews
_____ Presentations	_____ Questionnaires
_____ Individual and group projects	_____ Learning logs and journals

6. Who are the stakeholders and what is the level of their stakes in the assessment?

Stakeholder	Low Stake	Medium	High Stake
___ Students and parents			
___ Teachers			
___ Administrators			
___ Policy makers			
___ Colleges, employers			

7. How will cooperative learning be used to make the assessment more meaningful?

8. How will cooperative learning be used to make the assessment more manageable?

administrators, colleges, and employers. The assessment procedures may be criterion-referenced or norm-referenced. Last, the importance of assessment instruction and learning processes as well as outcomes is stressed; this is known as total-quality-learning.

Use the preceding reproducible form, "My Assessment Plan," to help think through and to map out your assessment approach for your classes.

CHAPTER 4

Using Groups for
Individual Assessment

I'm just a cowhand from Arkansas, but I have learned how to hold a team together. How to lift some men up, how to calm down others, until finally they've got one heartbeat together, a team. There's just three things I'd ever say: If anything goes bad, I did it. If anything goes semi-good, then we did it. If anything goes real good, then you did it. That's all it takes to get people to win football games for you.

Bear Bryant, former football
coach, University of Alabama

When James Watson and Francis Crick won a Nobel Prize for their discovery of the double helix, they both attributed their individual achievements to their collaboration with each other. Watson stated, "Nothing new that is really interesting comes without collaboration" (Watson, 1968). Crick stated, "Our . . . advantage was that we had evolved unstated but fruitful methods of collaboration . . . If either of us suggested a new idea, the other, while taking it seriously, would attempt to demolish it in a candid but nonhostile manner" (Watson, 1968). Thus their collaboration was based on a continuous assessment of each other's ideas and the stimulus to improve one's thinking. Individual achievements typically come from such cooperative systems, and cooperative groups can be used to assess the individual achievements of each member.

The basic purpose of a cooperative group is to make each member a stronger individual in his or her own right. Most assessments begin, therefore, with the teacher assessing the learning of group members as separate individuals. Groups are necessary for the assessment of many individual outcomes. There are myriad individual performances (such as mastery of social skills, singing in harmony, playing an instrument in concert with others, passing the ball to a teammate in basketball, giving an encouraging remark to a groupmate who is too shy to participate, expanding on a classmate's idea, giving good explanations, summarizing and integrating the views of others, criticizing the reasoning of another person) that can only be assessed within a group setting.

The assessment of individuals within groups begins with setting individual learning goals and involves such procedures as individual tests and products, observing students while the groups work, giving group members a questionnaire to complete, and interviewing group members during the group sessions. There is a pattern to classroom life summarized as "learn it in a group, perform it alone." The teacher may use the results of the individual assessments to structure the agenda for the next group session, and the group may use the individual assessments to provide remediation and further instruction of each member.

Assessment begins with setting goals. For individual assessment, goals must be set for each group members. Goals may be set within goal-setting conferences. Once goals are set, individual assessments may be conducted through tests, observing students as they work in groups, giving students questionnaires, and conducting individual interviews.

Setting Instructional and Learning Goals

If a man does not know to which port he is sailing, no wind is favorable.

Seneca

To assess individual students or a learning group, teachers must establish learning goals. A **goal** is a desired state of future affairs (Johnson & F. Johnson, 2002). An **individual goal** is future state of affairs desired by one person, whereas a **group goal** is a future state of affairs desired by enough members of a group to motivate the group to work towards its achievement. In establishing learning goals, teachers (1) set clear instructional objectives and (2) help students transform the instructional objectives into personal and group learning goals (Johnson & Johnson, 1996; 2002).

First, instructional goals must be formulated so they are (1) clearly understood by the teacher, students, and other interested parties and (2) can be assessed. The clarity and accessibility of goals depends on

Table 4.1   "START" With Goals

Goal Characteristic	Definition Of Characteristic
S: Specific	Goals have to be specific enough so that they are clearly understood and a plan to achieve them can be developed. Specific goals indicate what needs to be done next. General and ambiguous goals do not guide action.
T: Measurable and trackable	Students and the teacher must be able to determine the extent to which students have reached their learning goals. Goals must be operationalized so that the steps to achieving the goals are clear and understandable.
A: Challenging but achievable	Students' goals must be just beyond their current competence level. Ideally, the goals will be challenging enough that the student has a 50-50 percent chance of achieving them. Students' must be able to achieve the learning goals if they work hard enough and use the support systems available to help them do so.
R: Relevant	Learning goals must be relevant to the student's interests; the parent's concerns; the instructional goals of the teacher; and the national, state, district, and school standards. Students must see the goals as meaningful and be personally committed to achieving them.
T: Transfer	Learning goals must be aimed at having students take what is learned and transfer it to real-life situations. Whatever students learn today, they should be able to use in other situations tomorrow.

SOURCE: Reprinted with permission from: Johnson, D.W., & Johnson, R., (1996). *Meaningful and manageable assessment through cooperative learning.* Edina, MN: Interaction Book Company.

the extent to which they meet the START criteria (see Table 4.1). To be effective, goals need to be specific (so it is clear what needs to be done next), measurable (so progress can be tracked), challenging (offering a moderate risk of failure), relevant to students' interests, and aimed at competencies that will be transferred to real-life situations. The more that individual and group goals meet these criteria, the clearer the goals may be to students.

Second, the instructional goals must be transformed into learning goals. In educational settings, goals tend to be imposed on students. Students are required to learn how to read, how to do math, how to speak and write their language correctly, and how to be responsible citizens, whether they want to or not. An essential aspect of instruction is inducing students' commitment to what they are supposed to learn. Commitment is based on students understanding, accepting, and desiring to achieve instructional goals. Ways of inducing student commitment include involving students in the process of forming the learning goals. One way to facilitate this process is the goal-setting conference. A **goal-setting conference** is a meeting in which each student or group formulates learning goals, develops a contract to achieve them, and publicly commits himself or herself to achieving them. In a goal-setting conference, students reformulate instructional goals into personal learning goals, commit themselves to achieving them, and commit themselves to helping their groupmates learn. For many assignments, there are group goals as well as individual goals. The goal-setting conference clarifies the group goals as well as individual ones. See Table 4.2 for information about types of conferences.

There are four types of goal-setting conferences (Johnson & Johnson, 1996, 2002): (1) teacher-student (teacher conducts a goal-setting conference with each individual student), (2) teacher-group (teacher conducts a goal-setting conference with each cooperative learning group), (3) group (cooperative learning group conducts goal-setting conference with each member while the teacher supervises), and (4) group-to-group (one cooperative learning group conducts goal-setting conference with another group and its members while the teacher supervises). The three phases of the goal-setting conference are (1) preparing for the conference, (2) conducting the conference, and (3) following up on the conference. See Table 4.3.

The goals of individuals are related through social interdependence. There may be a positive correlation among individuals' goal attainment (i.e., cooperation), a negative correlation (i.e., competition), or no correlation (i.e., individualistic efforts). In group assignments and projects, clear positive interdependence must be structured among group members so they work cooperatively in achieving their joint goals. "My Learning Contract" outlines the goal-setting process from the students' view.

As we've stated, individual and group assessment begins by setting individual and group instructional goals and involving students and groups in clarifying and transforming the instructional goals into

Table 4.2   Types of Conferences

Conference	Individual Student	Cooperative Learning Group
Goal-setting conferences	Each class period, day, week, or instructional unit, each student sets personal learning goals and publicly commits him- or herself to achieve them in a learning contract.	Each class period, day, week, or instructional unit, each cooperative group sets group learning goals and members publicly commit themselves to achieve them in a learning contract.
Progress-assessment conferences	The student's progress in achieving his or her learning goals is assessed, what the student has accomplished so far and what is yet to be done is reviewed, and the student's next steps are detailed.	The group's progress in achieving its learning goals is assessed, what the group has accomplished so far and what is yet to be done is reviewed, and the group's next steps are detailed.
Postevaluation conferences	The student explains his or her level of achievement (what the student learned and failed to learn during the instructional unit) to interested parties (student's cooperative learning group, teachers, and parents), which naturally leads to the next goal-setting conference.	The group explains its level of achievement (what the group has accomplished and failed to accomplish during the instructional unit) to interested parties (members, teachers, and parents), which naturally leads to the next goal-setting conference.

SOURCE: Reprinted with permission from: Johnson, D.W., & Johnson, R., (1996). *Meaningful and manageable assessment through cooperative learning.* Edina, MN: Interaction Book Company.

Table 4.3   Goal-Setting Conferences

Step	Activity
1	Plan instructional unit.
2	Diagnose what student already knows.
3	Set learning goals.
4	Ensure that goals meet the START criteria.
5	Plan steps to achieving goals (process).
6	Identify resources needed for each step.
7	Make time line with resources identified.
8	Specify criteria for success.

SOURCE: Reprinted with permission from: Johnson, D.W., & Johnson, R., (1996). *Meaningful and manageable assessment through cooperative learning.* Edina, MN: Interaction Book Company.

My Learning Contract

My Academic Goals	My Responsibilities for Helping Others Learn	My Group's Goals
1.		
2.		
3.		
4.		

The plan for achieving my learning goals, meeting my responsibilities, and helping my group:

The time line for achieving my goals:

Beginning date:

First road mark:

Second road mark:

Third road mark:

Final Date:

Signatures:

_____   _____

_____   _____

SOURCE: Reprinted with permission from Johnson & Johnson (1996).

learning groups within conferences. Students then work to achieve these goals. Their progress and success in doing so are assessed in formative and summative procedures. Ways of doing so include tests, observations, and interviews.

Cooperative Learning and Teacher-Made Tests

Teachers may use learning groups to facilitate testing of students and the group as a whole in at least four ways: (1) group-individual-group procedure, (2) weekly group tests with an individual final exam, (3) group discussion tests, and (4) academic tournaments. Using these group procedures integrates testing into the instructional program and enhances learning.

Group Preparation, Individual Test, Group Test Procedure

You should frequently give quizzes and tests to assess (1) how much each student knows and (2) what students still need to learn. Whenever you give a test, cooperative learning groups can serve as bookends by preparing members to take the test and providing a setting in which students review the test. Two advantages in using cooperative learning groups in administrating tests are as follows (Johnson, Johnson, & Holubec, 1998b; Johnson, Johnson, & Smith, 1998). **First**, allowing students to work together before an assessment can level the playing field by enabling students to compare understandings and ensure that they all have the same background knowledge to prepare for the assessment. **Second**, allowing students to work in groups immediately following the assessment (1) allows each group member to discover what he or she did and did not understand, (2) allows each group member to discover where the information required to answer the questions is in the course materials, and (3) allows the group to provide remediation to members who did not understand the course content covered in the test.

The sequence of using cooperative learning groups in testing is as follows: (1) Students work together in cooperative learning groups to review the material to be covered in the test, (2) each student takes the test individually, and (3) students retake the test in the learning group (**Group Preparation, Individual Test, Group Test**). Using this procedure will result in (1) optimizing each student's preparation for the test, (2) making each student accountable to peers for his or her performance on the test, (3) assessing how much each student knows, (4) assessing what students still need to learn, (5) providing students with immediate clarification of what they did not understand or learn,

(6) providing students with immediate remediation of what they did not learn, (7) preventing arguments between you and your students over which answers are correct and why.

Preparing for a Test in Groups

Students prepare for, and review for, a test in learning groups that are heterogeneous in terms of achievement level in past performance. Students meet in their learning groups and are given study questions and class time to prepare for the examination. The task for students is to discuss each study question and come to a consensus about its answer. The cooperative goal is that all group members understand how to answer the study questions correctly. If students disagree on the answers to any study questions, they must find the page numbers and paragraphs in the resource material explaining the relevant information or procedures. When the study or review time is up, the students give each other encouragement for doing well on the upcoming test.

Taking the Test Individually

Each student takes the test individually, making two copies of his or her answers. The task (and individual goal) is to answer each test question correctly. Students submit one copy of the answers to you, the teacher, and keep one copy for group discussion. You score the answers and evaluate student performance against a preset criterion of excellence. If all members of the group score above a preset criterion (such as 90 percent correct) on the individual tests, then each member receives a designated number of bonus points (such as five). The bonus points are added to their individual scores to determine their individual grades for the test.

Retaking the Test in Groups

After all group members have finished taking the test individually, students meet in their learning groups to take the test again. The **task** is to answer each question correctly. The **cooperative goal** is to ensure that all group members understand the material and procedures covered by the test. Members do so by (1) reaching a consensus on the answer for each question and the rationale or procedure underlying the answer and (2) ensuring that all members can explain the answer and the rationale or procedure. The teacher randomly observes the groups to check that they are adhering to the following procedure:

1. Compare their answers on the first question.
   a. If they agree, one member explains the rationale or procedure underlying the question, and the other members check the explanation for accuracy. The group then moves on to question two.
   b. If they disagree, members must find the page number and paragraph in the resource materials explaining the relevant information or procedures. The group is responsible for ensuring that all members understand the material they missed on the test. Group members may assign review homework to each other if it is necessary. When all members agree on the answer and believe other members comprehend the material, the group moves on to question two.

2. Repeat this procedure until the group has covered all the test questions.

3. Celebrate how hard members have worked in learning the material and how successful they were on the test.

Weekly Group Tests and Individual Final Exam

During a course, students' higher-level reasoning and long-term retention may be maximized through the use of weekly group tests and an individual final exam. The weekly group test procedure is as follows: (1) Students are assigned to base groups of four members that are heterogeneous in terms of achievement level. (2) The groups complete the assignments together all week. (3) On Friday, a closed-book examination is given. Each group is divided into two pairs. Each pair takes the test without being able to refer to the texts or their notes. Their task is to reach agreement on the correct answer for each question. (4) When the two pairs are finished, the group of four meets and retakes the test as an open-book examination. On any question to which the two pairs have different answers or members are unsure of the answer, they find the page numbers and paragraphs in the textbook where the answer is explained (it is an open-book test). Each group is responsible for ensuring that all members understand the material they missed on the test. The group may assign review homework to members if it is necessary. The teacher randomly observes each group to ensure that they are answering the questions correctly. (5) Each group then hands in one answer sheet with a list of all members. Each member signs the answer sheet to verify that (a) he or she understands the content and (b) all other group members understand the content covered by the test. (6) All group members are given equal credit for successfully passing the test.

Each student takes an individual final examination at the end of the grading period. If any group member scores below a preset criterion (such as 90 percent), then the group meets and reviews the content with the member until the member can successfully pass the test. This rarely happens, as the group members have verified each week that they all are learning the assigned content.

Group Discussion Test

To make testing a higher-level learning experience, a group discussion procedure may be used. Students meet in their cooperative base group and discuss the content of the assigned readings and class sessions (Johnson, Johnson, & Holubec, 1998b). Students demonstrate mastery and deeper-level understanding of the course content while at the same time having an intellectually stimulating, creative, fun, and practically useful discussion. Within each group, members come to consensus about the answers to the test questions and ensure that all members are able to explain the answers. During the group test, group members should focus on the following:

- Integrating relevant theory, research, and practical experiences
- Analyzing possible answers to the question in depth to achieve insights into the issue
- Thinking divergently
- Critically examining each other's reasoning and engaging in constructive controversy
- Making the examination a fun and enjoyable experience for everyone

The test questions are broad in the sense of requiring the integration of material from many different chapters, books, and class sessions to create answers. Two examples of questions follow:

1. Your child is watching twenty hours of television per week. Many of the programs contain violence, racism, and sexism. Without turning off the TV, cite theories and research that might help you mediate the impact of TV on their attitudes and behavior.

2. You are a committee appointed by the president of the United States to develop a plan to ensure that all students within the public schools are socialized into a basic set of values and attitudes, such as honesty, hard work, persistence, achievement motivation, respect for others,

commitment to democracy, and desire to contribute to making our society (and world) a better place to live. What are your recommendations and why?

The group exam consists of five phases. First, each member chooses two of the suggested discussion questions and writes out an answer making sure the answer combines material from many different chapters of the assigned texts as well as his or her own relevant personal experiences and background.

Second, each member plans how to lead a group discussion on the question that will require higher-level reasoning, critical thinking, conceptual integration of material from many different chapters of the assigned texts and class sessions, and a working knowledge of the specific relevant theories and research findings. To facilitate the discussion, the member prepares an outline of the answer to the question with the relevant page numbers in the texts, copies of relevant written information from class sessions and other relevant sources, and visual aids, such as diagrams, charts, and cartoons.

Third, when the group meets for the discussion test, each member has prepared to lead discussions on two questions. The group discussion test should cover at least one question from each member. A coin is flipped to select the question that will be part of the examination. Each member then leads a discussion of the question selected. Time limits are set for each question, and a time keeper is appointed to ensure that the group sticks to the limits. During the discussion, group members are expected to do the following:

- Cite specific theories, research, and concepts discussed in the texts. Refer to specific pages. It is easy to make overly broad generalizations and to state personal opinions that are not supported by current knowledge.
- Refer to personal experiences. Comparing the theories and research findings against an individual's personal and practical experiences is valuable and often allows for integration of several concepts. But do not chat about "what happened to me."
- Encourage disagreement and controversy. All viewpoints and positions should be encouraged as long as they can be supported by theory and research. Follow the rules for constructive controversy.
- Ensure that all members participate actively to (a) contribute to the learning of others and (b) demonstrate overtly to the other members of the group that they have read the texts and mastered the content of the course.

Fourth, each member signs the Group Exam Certification Form to document that the criteria for passing were met by all group members. Each signature testifies that the member (a) arrived at the examination fully prepared, (b) participated actively in the discussion of each question, and (c) the other members did also. If any group member was absent, the group is to determine what the member has to do to make up the test.

Fifth and last, the group hands in a report consisting of the Group Exam Certification Form, a list of the questions discussed, and a summary of the answers and conclusions generated by the discussion. Groups may also add an evaluation of their experience.

Academic Tournament

As an alternative to an individual test, an **academic tournament** is an objective test (usually recognition or total-recall level) conducted in a game format (Johnson, Johnson, & Holubec, 1998a). A tournament is aimed at determining which learning group has best learned the assigned material. The tournament was developed by David DeVries and Keith Edwards (1974). An adaptation of their procedure is as follows:

1. Assign students to learning groups, ensuring that the members are of different achievement levels (one high-, two medium-, and one low-achieving student in each group). Group members complete the assignments together, ensure that each member masters the assigned material, and prepare each other for the tournament.

2. Assign students to competitive triads that are homogeneous by achievement levels. When students compete, they should be placed in homogeneous groups based on previous achievement. Rank the students in each cooperative learning group from highest to lowest on the basis of their previous achievement. Given that only one student from a group can be in a competitive triad, assign the three highest-achieving students in the class to Table 1, the next three to Table 2, and so on, until the three lowest-achieving students in the class are in the bottom table. Each student then competes as a representative of his or her learning group with students of equal achievement levels from other groups. Groups of three maximize the number of winners in the class (pairs tend to make the competition too personal). This creates equal competition within each triad and makes it possible for students of all achievement levels to contribute maximally to their team scores if they do their best. Figure 4.1 illustrates the relationship between the cooperative learning groups and the competitive triads.

Group Exam Certification Form.

We, the undersigned, certify that we have participated in the group discussion examination and have met the following criteria:

1. We understand the basic concepts, theories, and bodies of research presented in the texts and lectures.

2. We know the major theorists and researchers discussed in the texts and lectures.

3. We can apply the theories and research findings to practical situations.

4. We can conceptualize a research question and design a research study to test our hypotheses.

5. We have submitted our choice of questions and a brief summary of each answer we have formulated as a group.

Name	Signature	Date

SOURCE: Reprinted with permission from Johnson, Johnson, & Holubec (1998b).

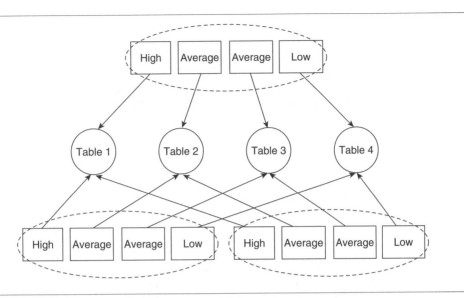

Figure 4.1   Assignment to Tournament Tables

SOURCE: Reprinted with permission from: Johnson, D.W., Johnson, R., & Holubec, E., (1998a). *Advanced cooperative learning* (3rd ed.). Edina, MN: Interaction Book Company.

3. Arrange the classroom. Separate the triads from each other, and have the students within each tournament triad sit close to each other.

4. Prepare instructional materials. The tournament has a game format. The game lasts from ten to thirty minutes. It requires a game sheet of about thirty items, a game answer sheet, and a copy of the rules. Make a set of cards numbered from 1 to 30. On each card, write (a) one question from the game sheet and (b) the number of the question on the answer sheet. The questions can be either recognition or recall questions.

5. Conduct the tournament. The aim of the tournament is to determine which cooperative learning group best learned the assigned material. Students compete for first, second, and third place in their triads. The procedure for playing the game is in the **Rules of Play Instruction Sheet** given below.

6. Determine the winning cooperative learning group. Each student can earn from six to two points in their tournament triad. Determine how many points each member should receive, have them return to their learning group, and add the scores of the members together to derive a group score. Group scores are then ranked and announced. The winning group is congratulated.

Tournament Rules of Play

This intergroup competition is being conducted to determine which learning group has best learned the assigned material. Each member of your learning group has been assigned to a different tournament triad and will be given points according to how well he or she has mastered the assigned material, compared to the other two members of the tournament triad. The points of the members of your learning group will be added together to determine a group score. The learning group with the most points wins.

1. You have been given a deck of specially constructed cards and an answer sheet. To start the game, shuffle the cards and place them face down on the table. Play is in a clockwise rotation. Three rotating roles are assigned to players (roles are rotated in a clockwise direction after each question):
   a. Question Reader: Player draws a card, reads it aloud.
   b. Answer Giver: Player decides whether or not to give an answer.
   c. Answer Checker: If an answer is given, the player reads the answer to the question from the answer sheet, regardless of whether the answer is challenged.

2. To play, the Question Reader takes the top card from the deck and reads it aloud. The Answer Giver has a choice of two responses:
   a. States being unsure of the answer. The two other students may then volunteer to answer the question (the Question Reader has the first chance to answer the question). If no one wants to answer, the card is placed on the bottom of the deck.
   b. Answers the question and asks if anyone wants to challenge the answer. The player on the Answer Giver's right has the first right of challenge.

3. If there is no challenge, the Answer Checker reads the answer on the answer sheet out loud.
   a. If correct, the Answer Giver keeps the card.
   b. If incorrect, the card is placed on the bottom of the deck.

4. If there is a challenge, the challenger gives an answer before the official answer is read.
   a. If the Answer Giver is correct, he or she keeps the card, and the challenger must give up one of his or her cards (which is placed on the bottom of the deck).
   b. If the Answer Giver is incorrect and the challenger is correct, the challenger keeps the card.
   c. If both the Answer Giver and the challenger are incorrect, then the card is placed on the bottom of the deck.

5. The roles are rotated after each question.

6. The game ends when there are no more cards in the deck. Players count their cards and determine who has the most, second most, and least cards. The ranking is converted into points.

Ranking	Points
First place	6 Points
Second place	4 Points
Third place	2 points
Two tie for first place	5 points each
Three tie for first place	4 points each
Two tie for second place	3 points each

SOURCE: Reprinted with permission from Johnson, Johnson, & Holubec (1998a).

Tournament Scoring Sheet

Tournament Triad: _____ Date: _____ Unit: _____

Write the names of the triad members in the top row of the table. For each question answered, place a plus (+) for each question the student gets right, and place a minus (-) for each question the student gets wrong. Total the number right for each member and rank the three members from who got the most questions right to who got the least questions right.

Question			
1.			
2.			
3.			
4.			
5.			
6.			
7.			
8.			
9.			
10.			
Total			

SOURCE: Reprinted with permission from Johnson, Johnson, & Holubec (1998a).

Observing

A third procedure for assessing the performance of individuals within a group setting is **direct observation**. Teachers observe students to see who is and who is not on task, looks puzzled, or is finished and waiting for his or her next assignment. **Observation** is the recording and describing of behavior as it occurs (Johnson & Johnson, 1996, 2002). Its **purpose** is to provide objective data about the following:

• **The quality of student performances.** Many student performances (such as giving a speech, playing tennis, providing leadership, helping a classmate, using higher-level reasoning, or drawing a picture) can only be assessed through observational methods.

• **The quality of the processes and procedures students use in completing assignments.** To improve continuously the process of learning, students must receive feedback concerning their actions in completing an assignment.

In using observation as an assessment tool, you first need to prepare:

1. Decide which student behaviors, actions, and skills are to be observed. You can observe students to determine whether they are on task or off task; assess learning outcomes, such as depth of understanding, level of reasoning, mastery of problem-solving procedures, and meta-cognitive thinking; and assess students' mastery of the interpersonal and small-group skills needed to work with others.

2. Decide who will be the observers: the teacher, students, visitors, or some combination of these.

3. Make a sampling plan. You may observe one learning group for the entire class period and collect information on every member, or you may observe each group for a few minutes and rotate through all the groups during one class period.

4. Construct an observation sheet. Observation sheets are used to tally and count the number of times a behavior, action, or event is observed in a specified time period. A structured observation form is created by (a) defining exactly what behaviors, actions, skills, or events are being observed (all observers have to be looking for the same thing), (b) determining the time period during which the data will be collected (minutes to weeks), (c) entering the actions to be observed in the first column (each action or skill is placed in a separate row; the

Observation Form A

Observer: _____ Date: _____ Grade: _____

Actions	Edythe	Keith	Dale	Total
Contributes ideas				
Encourages participation				
Checks for understanding				
Gives group direction				
Other:				
Total				

Being an Observer

1. Use one observation form for each group. Place a tally mark in the appropriate row and column when a student engages in one of the targeted actions. Look for patterns of behavior in the group. Do not worry about recording everything, but observe as accurately and rapidly as possible.

2. Make notes on the back of the observation form if something takes place that should be shared with the group but does not fit into the actions being observed.

3. Write down specific positive and important contributions by each group member (to ensure that every member will receive positive feedback).

4. After the learning session is over, total the columns and rows. Transfer the totals to long-term record sheets and the appropriate charts or graphs. The observation forms should be dated and kept to assess the growth of the students and groups. When a group is observed more than once during a class session, different colored inks may be used. This allows group members to assess their skill development at a glance.

5. Give the information gathered to the group, and assist group members in deriving conclusions. Show the observation form to the group, holding it so all members can see it. Ask the group, "*What do you conclude about (a) your participation in the group and (b) the group functioning in general?*" Ensure that all group members receive positive feedback about their efforts to learn and help their groupmates learn. After small-group processing, there is whole-class processing.

6. Help group members set goals for improving their competence in engaging in the social skills during the next group meeting by asking, "*What could you add to be an even better group tomorrow than you were today?*" Have members discuss the goals and publicly commit to achieving them. Emphasize the continuous improvement of students' competencies and group effectiveness.

SOURCE: Reprinted with permission from Johnson, Johnson, & Holubec (1998a).

final row is reserved for the total of the columns), (d) making an additional column for each member of the group, (e) making a final column to record the total for each row on the form, and (f) making sure all columns are clearly labeled and wide enough to enter data. See Observation Forms A and B as samples. The sidebar, "Five-Minute Walk," outlines the process.

5. Train the observers to follow observation procedures, use the observation forms, and follow the sampling plan.

Next, observe and record how each student performs the specified behaviors.

Then, summarize the observations in a clear and useful manner and give feedback to each student and group. Help students analyze the observation data and reflect on how effectively they are learning and helping each other learn and how they may behave more effectively next time. Charts are helpful to display the results of observations so that students, parents, and other interested parties may interpret them. Students should receive feedback on the quality of their efforts to learn and help classmates learn so they can continuously improve both. **Feedback** in this context is information on actual performance that individuals compare with criteria for ideal performance. When feedback is given skillfully, it generates energy, directs it toward constructive action, and transforms it into action for improving the performance of teamwork skills. The results may include a decrease in the discrepancy between actual and real performance, increased self-efficacy, and empowerment to be even more effective next time. (The Feedback Checklist may help in assessing the effectiveness of feedback.) Provide a time and structure for students to reflect on and analyze the quality of their efforts to learn and help classmates learn and to make decisions about what actions to continue or change. Last, make time and opportunity for students to celebrate their hard work and success.

Questionnaires

A fourth procedure for assessing the performance of individual group members is the use of questionnaires. In constructing a questionnaire, you decide on what types of questions to use and which forms of response to elicit, write well-worded questions, arrange the questions into the optimal sequence, and ensure that the physical layout is appealing and facilitates the ease with which the questionnaire may be completed and scored (Johnson & Johnson, 1996, 2002).

Observation Form B

Observer: _____ **Date:** _____ **Grade:** _____

Assignment: _____

Directions for use: (1) Put the names of the group members above each column. (2) Put a tally mark in the appropriate box each time a group member contributes. (3) Make notes on the back when interesting things happen that are not captured by the categories. (4) Write down one (or more) positive contribution made by each group member.

Action					Total
Contributes ideas					
Describes feelings					
Encourages participation					
Summarizes, integrates					
Checks for understanding					
Relates new to old learning					
Gives direction to work					
Total					

SOURCE: Reprinted with permission from Johnson, Johnson, & Holubec (1998a).

Five-Minute Walk

1. Select actions to observe.

2. Construct observation sheet.

3. Plan route through the classroom.

4. Gather data on every group.

5. Give feedback on the data to the groups or the class as a whole.

6. Chart or graph the results.

Constructing a Questionnaire

In preparing a questionnaire, three types of questions can be used: open-ended, closed-ended, and semantic-differential questions (Johnson & Johnson, 1996, 2002). **Open-ended questions** require students to answer by writing a statement that may vary from a free response to a word or phrase to filling in the blanks. Examples of open-ended questions:

Feedback Checklist

Feedback	Yes	No, Start Over
Is feedback given?		Was not given or received; start over
Is feedback generating energy in students?		Students are indifferent; start over
Is energy directed toward identifying and solving problems so performance is improved?		Energy used to resist, deny, avoid feedback; start over
Do students have opportunities to take action to improve performance?		No, students are frustrated and feel like failures; start over

SOURCE: Reprinted with permission from: Johnson, D. W., Johnson, R., & Holubec, E., (1998a). *Advanced cooperative learning* (3rd ed.). Edina, MN: Interaction Book Company.

What is your most challenging subject? Please explain why.

My general opinion about math is _____.

My teachers are _____.

If someone suggested I take up math as my life's work, I would reply
_____.

Math is my _____ subject.

Student responses may be scored by counting the number of times a word or phrase occurs. Mean and standard deviations may then be calculated. Open-ended questions, however, tend to be hard to analyze and often are not fully answered.

Closed-ended questions require the student to indicate the alternative answer closest to his or her internal response. The choices can be dichotomous, multiple choice, ranking, or scale. Here are some examples:

Math is my favorite school subject. ___ True ___ False

Do you intend to take another course in Math?
___ Yes ___ No ___ Don't Know

Circle each of the words that tell how you feel about Math:
interesting   very important   worthless   difficult   dull
weird   exciting   boring   useful

Rank these subject areas from least interesting (1) to most interesting (6) to you:

_____ Social Studies   _____ English
_____ Science   _____ Mathematics
_____ Math   _____ Foreign Language

How interested are you in learning more about Math? Circle the number that best represents your degree of interest.

Very Uninterested 1---2---3---4---5---6---7 Very Interested

The questions are scored by counting the frequencies of each response and then calculating the mean response and the standard deviation.

Perhaps the most general method for the measurement of attitudes is **the semantic differential** (Osgood, Suci, & Tannenbaum, 1957). This type of question allows the teacher to present any object or concept (be it a person, issue, practice, subject area, or anything else) and obtain an indication of student responses toward it. A semantic-differential question consists of a series of rating scales of bipolar adjective pairs listed underneath the concept the teacher wishes to obtain student attitudes toward. Here is an example:

History

Ugly 1---2---3---4---5---6---7 Beautiful

Bad 1---2---3---4---5---6---7 Good

Worthless 1---2---3---4---5---6---7 Valuable

Negative 1---2---3---4---5---6---7 Positive

The teacher then sums the responses to obtain an overall indication of attitudes toward the concept. Almost any concept of interest can be used in this type of question. Each concept is listed separately with the same sets of adjectives underneath. If a teacher does not use adjective pairs that are generally evaluative, such as those given above, he or she may wish to score the responses to each adjective pair separately instead of summing them.

How Good Are Your Questions?

Writing good closed-ended and open-ended questions takes some expertise and practice. After writing a set of questions, you may evaluate each question by considering the following points (Johnson & Johnson, 1996, 2002):

- Are all the words in the question familiar to the respondents?
- Is the question worded without slang phases, colloquialisms, and bureaucratic words?
- Is the question worded simply, with no abbreviations and difficult words?
- Does the question ask for only one piece of information? (Not: Rate the quality and relevance of this class.)
- Are any words emotionally loaded, vaguely defined, or overly general?
- Do any words have a double meaning that may cause misunderstandings (e.g., liberal, conservative, traditional)?
- Is only one adjective or adverb used in the question? (Not: Is the teacher helpful and sensitive?)
- Does the wording of the question imply a desired answer?
- Are the response options mutually exclusive and sufficient to cover each conceivable answer?
- Does the question contain words that tend not to have a common meaning, such as significant, always, usually, most, never, and several?

Decisions Regarding Form of Responses to Questions

As we've mentioned, there are two general types of responses (Johnson & Johnson, 1996, 2002): open-ended responses or closed-ended responses. The types of open-ended responses are fill-in-the-blank and free responses. The types of closed-ended responses include dichotomous, multiple choice, ranking, or scale. One of the most common approaches for writing closed-ended questions with a scaled response is the **Likert method of summated ratings**. The procedure for developing a Likert scale is to ask several questions about the topic of interest. For each question, a response scale is given, with anywhere from three to nine points. Questions with five alternatives are quite common. Two ways of presenting the alternatives are shown as follows:

_____ Strongly disagree (1)   _____ Agree (4)

_____ Disagree (2)   _____ Strongly agree (5)

_____ Undecided (3)

Strongly disagree 1---2---3---4---5 Strongly agree

A student's responses for all the questions are summed together to get an overall score indicating the student's attitudes toward the issue being measured. The results for an entire class or school may be factor analyzed to build an attitude scale consisting of more than three items.

Question Sequence

A questionnaire (or interview) consists of a series of question sequences (Johnson & Johnson, 1996, 2002). The order of the sequences must be arranged so that responses are unbiased. In ordering your questions, you may wish to use the funnel sequence with various filter questions. The **funnel sequence** starts off with broad questions and then progressively narrows down the scope of the questions until very specific questions are asked at the end. A **filter question** is used to exclude a respondent from a particular sequence of questions if the questions are not relevant to him or her. For instance, you wish to ask for some factual information about a history class; obviously, if the student is not taking history, there is no point in asking for specifics about that class. In a questionnaire (or interview), try to avoid (1) putting ideas into respondents' minds and (2) suggesting that they have attitudes when they do not. With any issue, you will want to start with open questions and only introduce more structured questions in a later stage. See "My Participation in Cooperative Groups" for an example.

Interviewing

The fifth procedure for assessing individual students in a group context is interviewing (Johnson & Johnson, 1996, 2002). An **interview** is a personal interaction in which verbal questions are asked and verbal or linguistic responses are given between the interviewer (the teacher) and one or more interviewees (students). The interviewer has the opportunity to observe both the student and the total situation to which the student is responding. A teacher may interview any student of any age or ability level. Interviews may involve one student or a small group of students and they may take place before, during, and after a lesson or instructional unit. The key problem with interviewing is the subjective nature of asking questions and recording student responses.

There are a number of advantages to conducting interviews while students are working in groups. First, the interviewer and the respondents are face to face, and therefore, questions and answers can be clearly communicated, and misunderstandings can be identified and

My Participation in Cooperative Groups

Name: _____ Date: _____ Class: _____

1. When I knew an answer or had an idea, I shared it with the group.
   Never 1---2---3---4---5 Always [for consistency]

2. When my answer did not agree with someone else's, I tried to find out why.
   Never 1---2---3---4---5 Always

3. When I did not understand something, I asked others to explain.
   Never 1---2---3---4---5 Always

4. When someone else did not understand, I explained it until he or she did.
   Never 1---2---3---4---5 Always

5. I tried to make the people in the group feel appreciated and respected.
   Never 1---2---3---4---5 Always

6. Before I signed my name to our paper, I made sure that I understood everything, agreed with the answers, and was confident that all other members understood the answers.
   Never 1---2---3---4---5 Always

SOURCE: Reprinted with permission from Johnson, Johnson, and Holubec (1998b).

immediately clarified. Second, the learning of preschool and primary students who cannot read or write can be assessed in an interview. Third, **oral examinations**, that is, interviewing students about what they are learning, provide a much more valid and reliable assessment of the progress of students who have learning disabilities that impair their ability to read or write (such as dyslexia). Fourth, interviews give teachers control over the assessment situation, as a student response may determine what question the teacher asks next. The sequence of questions may be modified according to the responses given by the student.

Fifth, interviews can teach as well as assess. Interviewing creates an opportunity to teach students their own wisdom. By adapting questions to the specific answers students are giving, the teacher can help students to (a) reflect on what they know, (b) clarify their reasoning, (c) reconceptualize and reorganize what they are learning, (d) develop new and more refined levels of understanding, (e) believe their ideas are valued, (f) be pleased about their progress, and (g) set future goals. The Socratic method of teaching, for example, is an oral interview in which the inconsistencies and conflicts in a student's reasoning are highlighted in order to lead students to deeper and deeper insights about what they know.

Interviewing is a unique assessment procedure as it allows teachers to assess what students know and understand while at the same time teaching students by stimulating reflection and reconceptualization. The face-to-face, direct interaction gives the teacher more opportunity to guide students in their interpretations of the questions, ensure that students supply accurate and complete information, reveal the complexity of students' reasoning, clarify what the students are trying to communicate, probe for students' attitudes and beliefs, and motivate students to do their best. Interviewing may be the most flexible procedure for simultaneously assessing and teaching students. It may also give teachers the most control over the assessment situation.

The greatest strength of the interview may be the opportunity it provides to build positive relationships between the teacher and the students. Through the direct, face-to-face interaction inherent in interviewing, the teacher gets to know the students better (both personally and academically); build rapport with the students; establish norms about the teacher-student relationship; and create more personal, positive, supportive, and trusting relationships with the students. The learning climate of the class and school becomes more positive and powerful as teacher-student relationships become more supportive.

Types of Questions

Interviews are often structured according to whether they contain fixed-alternative (closed-ended) and open-ended questions (Johnson & Johnson, 1996, 2002).

Fixed-Alternative Questions

Fixed-alternative or closed-ended questions are used when the possible alternative answers are known, limited, and clear (*History class is enjoyable.* _____ *Yes* _____ *No*). Closed-ended questions are very useful in obtaining factual information and knowledge, as they (1) are easy to develop and administer, (2) are quick and inexpensive to analyze, (3) are easy to understand, (4) eliminate the possibility of irrelevant answers, and (5) require the respondent, not the interviewer, to make judgments. On the other hand, they may (1) not include important alternative responses, (2) include alternatives that are interpreted differently by various respondents, and (3) force respondents to give answers that do not reflect their true knowledge or opinion.

Open-Ended Questions

Open-ended **questions** are used when the subject is complex, when relevant aspects are not known, or when the objective of the interview is to explore students' knowledge and reasoning processes. Simply asking a student to explain what he or she knows is perhaps the best way to determine whether a student understands a subject or problem. Open-ended questions have the advantages of (1) not biasing responses by suggesting alternatives, (2) eliciting information on students' reasoning, and (3) providing the opportunity to clarify and probe a student's response. On the other hand, open-ended questions (1) may be difficult to administer, (2) require extensive training of the interviewer, and (3) elicit responses that are complex and difficult to analyze.

How to Interview Students

There are at least three types of interviews commonly used by teachers (Johnson & Johnson, 1996, 2002): random oral exams, focused interviews, and small-group interviews.

Random Oral Exam

While students are working on an assignment, particular checks on what is being learned can be done through individual oral exams. There are two procedures for doing so:

- You can move from group to group, randomly choosing one student from each group to explain (a) what he or she has learned so far and (b) how the group is proceeding to complete the assignment.
- You can give each group a number and give each member a letter. You randomly draw numbers and letters out of a hat to ask an individual student to explain the answer to a question. Thus if you have ten groups of three students each, the groups are numbered from one to ten and the members are lettered from A to C. You might randomly draw Group 7, Person B. You would then ask that person to give the answer to a question. If he or she cannot do so, the other two Group 7 members may give the person help until he or she is able to answer the question adequately.

Focused Interview

In a **focused interview,** the teacher arranges questions like a funnel so that the initial questions are broad and general and subsequent questions require the student to be more and more precise and specific in his or her answers. This gives the interviewer the freedom to explore and probe in directions that are unanticipated before beginning the

Interviewing Students to Assess Reasoning

Class: _____ Date: _____

	Group 1	Group 2	Group 3	Group 4
What are you doing?				
Why are you doing it?				
How will it help you?				

interview. Since the subsequent questions are built on the statements made by the student being interviewed, only the initial questions are planned. Each student is given a different interview as each follow-up question is idiosyncratic to the student's previous response. The teacher may ask, for example, for the student's analysis of *Heart of Darkness* by Joseph Conrad and, according to what the student says in response, ask a series of questions that require the student to reveal more and more of his or her impressions of and reasoning about the novel. See "Interviewing Students to Assess Reasoning."

Small-Group Interview

Small-group interviews are used to assess whether all group members have mastered and understood the assigned material. Conducting small-group interviews begins with giving each group a set of questions and instructing the groups to prepare all group members to respond to each question. Choose a group, randomly select one member to explain the answer to a randomly selected question, ask other members to add to the answer when that member finishes responding to the question, and judge the final answer to be adequate or inadequate. You then ask another member a different question and repeat the procedure until all questions have been answered or until you (the teacher) judge all members of the group to be adequately prepared. If the group members cannot answer the questions, you ask the group to return to the questions until members are better prepared. You may give the group guidance by identifying particular weaknesses and strengths of the members' answers. The group members are given equal credit for successfully passing the test. Small-group interviews allow you to quickly sample students' level of learning while making personal contact with each student. On the other hand, the group may have an inhibiting influence on some individuals, and a chaining effect may occur that biases responses. See Guidelines for Interviewing.

Guidelines for Interviewing

1. Word and organize the questions so that the relationship between you and the student becomes more positive and trusting. A positive, trusting relationship encourages both you and the student to feel at ease, be spontaneous, respond honestly, and communicate effectively.

2. Phrase questions so that (a) students do not become defensive, (b) students' thoughts are clarified, (c) students have the opportunity to expand or modify, (d) you do not put ideas into a student's mind, and (e) you do not suggest that students have attitudes when they have none.

3. Begin the interview with simple, nonthreatening questions, and save the more complex and threatening questions for the end of the interview.

4. Move from general to specific questions.

5. Make nonverbal cues helpful to eliciting full and complete responses from the student. Avoid smiling too much and excessive affirmative nodding of the head.

6. Be quiet. What the student needs is a skillful, empathetic listener.

7. Allow sufficient wait time for students to formulate their thoughts and answers. Do not rush students' responses.

8. The questions asked should prompt students to give information previously learned or collected, add to their answers, put a sequence of ideas together, provide evidence for their conclusions, and apply known concepts to new situations.

SOURCE: Reprinted with permission from: Johnson, D. W., & Johnson, R., (1996). *Meaningful and manageable assessment through cooperative learning.* Edina, MN: Interaction Book Company.

Improving Homework Through Groups

Teachers may improve the quantity and quality of completed homework by beginning each class session with having a cooperative base group assess the quality of each member's homework (Johnson, Johnson, & Holubec, 1998b). The group's task (and cooperative goal) is to ensure that all members have completed the homework, brought it to class, and understood how to do it correctly. The expected criterion for success is for all group members to understand how to complete each part of the assignment correctly. The procedure is as follows:

1. At the beginning of class, students meet in cooperative base groups.

2. One member of each group, **the runner**, goes to the teacher's desk, picks up the group's folder, and hands out any materials in the folder to the appropriate members.

3. The group reviews the assignment step by step to determine how much of the assignment each member completed and how well each member understood how to complete the material covered. Two roles are used: **Explainer** (explains step by step how the homework is correctly completed) and **accuracy checker** (verifies that the explanation is accurate, encourages, and provides coaching if needed). The role of explainer is rotated so that each member takes turns explaining step by step how a portion of the homework is correctly completed. The other members are accuracy checkers. The base groups concentrate on clarifying the parts of the assignment that one or more members have not understood.

4. At the end of the review, the runner records how much of the assignment each member completed, places members' homework in the group's folder, and returns the folder to the teacher's desk.

To ensure that the group is successful, regular examinations are given, and each day, a group member is randomly selected to explain how to solve problems from the homework, also randomly selected.

An alternative procedure is to assign students to pairs, randomly pick questions from the homework assignment, and have one student explain the correct answer step by step. The other student listens, checks for accuracy, and prompts the explainer if he or she does not know the answer. Roles are switched for each question.

Summary

The basic purpose of a cooperative group is to make each member a stronger individual in his or her own right. When students work in groups, there are opportunities for assessment that never occur when students work by themselves. One focus of group assessment, therefore, is the individual performance of each group member.

Assessment begins with setting goals. Teachers may simply impose learning goals on students from their position of power and authority ("In this unit, you will learn the causes of the Civil War."), but students are far more motivated to achieve their personal goals than they are to achieve imposed instructional goals. Assessment involves three types of conferences with each student: A **goal-setting conference** to establish a contract containing the student's learning goals, **progress assessment conferences** to determine the student's progress in achieving his or her goals, and a **postevaluation conference** in which the student's accomplishments are explained to interested parties. The goal-setting conference may be between the teacher and the student, the teacher and the cooperative learning group, the cooperative learning group and the student, and a cooperative learning group and another group. In all cases, the emphasis is on helping students set and take ownership for learning goals that meet the START criteria (*S*pecific, *T*rackable, *A*chievable, *R*elevant, *T*ransferable). The goal-setting conference contains four steps: diagnosis of current level of expertise, setting START goals, organizing support systems and resources to help each student achieve his or her goals successfully, and constructing a plan for using the resources to achieve the goals and formalizing the plan into a learning contract.

A second way to assess the performance of individual group members is through individual objective or essay tests. Tests may be used to assess student learning, guide student learning, and guide instruction. Four of the ways that tests can be used as cooperative experiences are the group-individual-group testing procedure, weekly group tests with an individual final exam, group discussion tests, and academic tournaments.

A third way to assess the performance of individual group members is through observation aimed at recording and describing behavior as it occurs. Using observation as an assessment tool requires that teachers prepare for observing; know how to observe; and know how to summarize and organize the data for use by students, parents, and other stake-holders. Preparing for observing involves deciding what actions to observe, who will observe, and what the sampling plan will be; constructing an observation form; and training observers to use the form. Conducting observations may focus on students' on-task behavior, academic efforts, or social skills. In summarizing observations, the data may be displayed in charts, feedback is then given to students, students reflect on the feedback and set improvement goals.

A fourth way to assess the performance of individual group members is through the use of questionnaires. A questionnaire may contain open-ended, closed-ended, or semantic-differential questions. Each question needs to be well worded and requiring either an open-ended (fill-in-the-blank or free response) or closed-ended (dichotomous, multiple choice, ranking, or scale) responses. The questions are then arranged in an appropriate sequence and given an attractive format.

A fifth way to assess the performance of individual group members is through interviews. An **interview** is a personal interaction between a teacher and either one student or a small group of students, in which verbal questions are asked and verbal responses are given. Students may be interviewed before, during, and after a lesson or instructional unit. Interviews can contain fixed-alternative or open-ended questions. It is a highly flexible procedure that can be used for both assessment and teaching purposes. Students can be interviewed to assess their learning, cognitive reasoning, meta-cognitive thought, and retention. Students can also be interviewed to clarify their thinking, achieve new levels of understanding, reflect on their learning, believe their ideas are valued, appreciate their progress, and set future goals. Socrates is an example of a teacher who used oral interviews as a major instructional strategy. Interviews can also be used to build a more positive, supportive, and trusting relationship with each student.

CHAPTER 5

Assessing Groups as a Whole

I n the early 1920s at the University of Berlin, Kurt Lewin's students formed a close-knit group that met regularly to discuss psychological issues. Norman Maier (as quoted in Marrow, 1969) described the meetings as follows:

> The interaction between Lewin and his group of students was so free, and the disagreement so intense, that I remember them as the most stimulating experiences I have ever had....These were creative discussions during which ideas and theories were generated, explored, and controverted. (p. 36)

These discussions might go on for hours, often with shifting membership, and they often resulted in productive, exciting, and ultimately influential ideas whose source was truly the group, as no one could identify any one person as the idea's source. The discussion might take off from a more or less casual question or notion, be changed by one set of comments, qualified by another, reoriented by another set of comments, and could catch fire in still another exchange. What emerged might only be remotely related to the remark that had set off the discussion in the first place (Marrow, 1969).

In many situations, groups produce a product that may be assessed. In science classes, students work together to conduct an experiment. In drama classes, plays are presented. In physical education classes, teams compete. In social studies classes, a field study on the history of the area may be undertaken. When structured effectively, group products can significantly increase the learning of all group members. Group projects can be a powerful force to integrate the personal aims of students from nonacademic backgrounds into academic pursuits (Herrington & Curtin, 1990) and to broaden students' perspectives and generate new questions and problems (Dysthe, 1996; Short & Burke, 1991). Teachers plan the project and the assessment, observe students working together, set norms and teach teamwork skills, involve students in creating the criteria and rubrics needed for assessment, and involve students in assessing the quality of the group products. Group assignments need to be structured so that the requirement of a single product is carefully integrated with the conditions for effective group work and is seen as fair and beneficial by the students. In assessing a group, it is often difficult to determine who did what, because good ideas often emerge out of group interaction rather than out of any one particular contributor. In the long run, however, it becomes clear who sustains a record of productivity, whether as an individual or in contributing to group efforts.

As stated earlier, the usual rule for cooperative learning groups is that students learn in a group and are subsequently assessed as individuals (Johnson, Johnson, & Holubec, 1998b). While individual assessment is more common than group assessment in schools, in real life, it may be just the opposite. In most organizations, the success of the organization as a whole, the success of divisions in the organization, and the success of teams in the division are focused on more frequently than is the success of each individual employee. Authentic assessment, therefore, most often means group assessment.

In this chapter, the procedures for conducting group projects are reviewed, the teacher's role in assessing projects is discussed, and a variety of ways of assessing projects are presented. Involving students in constructing rubrics to assess the quality of the results of the project is discussed. Four specialized types of group projects are discussed: case studies, problem-based learning, group investigation, and coop-coop (intragroup and intergroup cooperation). The use of presentations as one result of a group project is discussed. First, however, the problems in assigning group products are reviewed.

Problems in Assigning Group Products

Assignments that result in a group product need to be structured so that (1) the requirement of a single product is carefully integrated with the conditions for effective group work, and (2) the assessment and evaluation of the group product is seen as fair and beneficial by the students. Many students have had unpleasant experiences working on poorly structured group projects. Many teachers have had frustrating experiences with groupwork not accomplishing its desired goals. Here follow some common problems:

- Students' workloads are very uneven so that some students do most of the work while others do very little. Social loafing is a common complaint made by students who work in groups (Lejk, Wyvill, & Farrow, 1996).
- Students are uncertain about how good is good enough, since views about quality typically vary widely.
- Group members are placed in opposition to each other and the group as a whole through the use of norm-referenced (as opposed to criterion-referenced) evaluation. In a criterion-referenced procedure, absolute criteria are set (95 percent for an A), and anyone and everyone who meets or exceeds this criterion receives that grade. It is possible for everyone (or no one) to get an A. In a norm-referenced procedure, such as grading on the curve, student performances are compared with one another, ranked, and given A–F grades relative to one another. No matter how good or poorly the students perform in an absolute sense, there are fixed percentages of each grade category. Norm-referenced grading is often assumed to be the norm in education, especially for high school and college, but a national survey conducted by Astin (1993) indicates only about 22 percent of all college faculty use norm-referenced procedures. One of the most common reasons that groupwork fails is that faculty put students in a fundamentally incompatible situation—being assigned to work together cooperatively on projects (and perhaps share a grade) and then being pitted against one another by grading them on the curve at the end of the course.
- The purposes of the project are unclear or poorly understood by the students. Teachers should ensure that there are good reasons for assigning a group product (complex task, multiple perspectives, divisible responsibilities, and so forth); that is, the instructional goals should clearly specify that a cooperative group is required to complete the project.
- Insufficient time is given to complete the project. Teachers should ensure that students are given sufficient time to accomplish the task successfully.

These and other problems with groupwork can be eliminated through carefully structuring cooperation and using diagnostic, formative, and summative assessments.

Carefully Structuring Group Work

Carefully structuring the five basic elements of cooperation into groups was discussed in Chapter 2. Positive interdependence must be clearly established so that all group members realize that they can succeed only if the other members of their group succeed. Students must realize that either they succeed together or they fail separately. Each student must be held individually accountable to contribute his or her fair share of the work. Students must promote the success of their group members through encouragement, help, sharing, and assistance. Students must possess the necessary social skills and experience in using them, to create successful group efforts. Group members must periodically process how well they are working together and how the effectiveness of the group may be improved. Each of these elements of effective cooperation must be clearly structured within the project groups. See "Create a Project" for an outline form useful in planning group project assignments.

Using Diagnostic, Formative, and Summative Assessments

Assessing the quality of students' groupwork is a summative activity, but the activity is made easier when diagnostic and formative assessments are built into the process. Before the project, a questionnaire can be given to each student to find out what students know about the area being studied and the process of completing a group project. During the project, formative assessments can be conducted by having students submit progress reports on how they are proceeding and what progress they are making. In addition, the teacher can observe the groups working on the projects during class to identify how effectively they are proceeding and to ensure that all group members are contributing and doing their fair share of the work. Last, the teacher can interview the group as a whole or selected group members to determine how the group is progressing.

Nature of Projects

Involving students in projects is a critical component of instruction in most subject areas (Johnson & Johnson, 1996, 2002). A **project** is an assignment aimed at having students produce something on a topic related to the curriculum rather than just reproduce knowledge on tests. Projects may be assigned at any grade level in any subject area. Projects may involve reports, presentations, experiments, models, maps, pictures, tables, graphs, collages, photographs, plays, films, or videotapes. The assignments can be aimed at enhancing communication, reasoning, technical, interpersonal, organizational, decision-making, and problem-solving skills. Projects may be completed by individual students, cooperative learning groups, whole classes, schools, and communities. Projects may involve both in-class and

Create a Project

1. List the projects you will assign students during the course:

   a.

   b.

   c.

   d.

2. Selecting one of the projects you listed, write out the steps you will follow in assigning the project:

   a.

   b.

   c.

   d.

   e.

   f.

   g.

out-of-class research and work. Projects allow students to be creative, use multiple modes of learning, and explore their own multiple intelligences. The disadvantages of projects are that they are difficult to assess and to store.

Why Use Projects

Despite the assessment challenges posed by projects, they can achieve objectives that may not be achieved in any other way:

- They require students to use, integrate, apply, and transfer a wide variety of diverse information and skills into a final product.
- They challenge students to engage in procedures (such as scientific investigation and inquiry) that promote higher-level outcomes.
- They make visible the methodology, values, and intellectual stance of the discipline.
- They powerfully demonstrate how knowledge is used in a field.
- They integrate personal purposes with academic learning.
- They allow students to be creative and inventive in integrating diverse knowledge and skills.
- They allow students to demonstrate and clarify their multiple intelligences through the use of diverse medias and the use of knowledge in real settings.
- They give students the opportunity to formulate their own questions and then try to answer them.
- They accommodate different achievement levels by allowing students to complete projects at varying levels of difficulty.

Take a look at "Examples of Projects" to spark your creativity.

General Steps for Assigning Projects

The wide variety of meaningful outcomes achieved by projects makes them a valuable and flexible teacher tool. Their richness and complexity make them ideally suited for cooperative learning groups. Teachers should assign a variety of projects throughout the academic year. The projects should be structured so that students (1) have some choice in the focus or topic of their projects; (2) can use a variety of competencies and intelligences in completing them; (3) have to use higher-level reasoning skills, such as induction and problem solving; and (4) can be creative and divergent in their approach to the assignment. Given below are the steps for assigning a project (Johnson & Johnson, 1996, 2002):

Examples of Projects

Create a mythological rap song: Write and present a rap song about the gods and goddesses in Greek mythology	**Select and research a disease and prepare an instructional pamphlet to present to the class.**
Select a famous writer, artist, politician, or philosopher from the Renaissance period and become that person on a panel of experts.	Research an international conflict in the world today (for each country, a student researches a different aspect of the country related to the war: history, resolutions, maps, and so forth.)
Teach growing cycles through gardening (different students are in charge of seeds, fertilizing, and so forth.)	**Paint a mural of the history of the earth and humankind (each group takes a section—Greek, Roman, middle ages, etc.).**
Videotape a community project.	Create a time line (personal, historical, literary, art, geological).
Write plays, skits, role plays.	**Produce a school or class newspaper.**
Run a school post office.	Present a mock court.
Plan and run an international festival, with multicultural activities.	**Paint a mural based on reading.**
Have groups write alternative endings to stories or novels, with dramatizations.	Create a new invention using the computer.
Turn a short story or event in history into a movie.	**Design an ideal school and enact it.**
Present a newscast.	Develop science fair projects.

1. For each project, teachers should give students a clear description of the project, its purposes, and how it will be conducted.

2. Teachers create a time line. For each project, the dates are listed for when the project starts, when each part of the project should be completed, when an initial draft is to be submitted for peer editing and initial teacher reaction, and when the final product is due.

3. Teachers show students samples or models of completed projects. A variety of projects ranging in quality from excellent to poor

helps students develop a frame of reference for what is and is not an acceptable finished product.

4. Teachers involve students in developing specific criteria to assess the quality of the completed projects. The criteria may include timeliness, appearance, originality, quality, evidence, reflection, richness of ideas, and presentation. Students develop indicators of excellent, medium, and inadequate products. If students want to make a video, for example, they can view several videos and then develop a rating scale that differentiates high-quality from medium and low-quality videos. The best video they view can be a benchmark to which they aspire. Students need to understand the components of a good project and then use indicators to guide them in their work.

5. Teachers supply and teach students a rubric that is standardized for the school, district, or state. Learning a standardized rubric to use in assessing the quality of projects gives students a more sophisticated frame of reference to use in reflecting on their own work.

6. Students are assigned to cooperative learning groups. The required materials, equipment, and other resources are provided. The group completes the project with help and assistance from faculty, ensuring that all members have contributed their fair share of the work, can explain its content and how it was conducted, and can explain the results.

7. Teachers have students present their completed projects to some or all of their classmates. Either each group member presents an equal part of the report or else each member presents the entire report to a section of the class. In viewing classmates' projects, students use the rating scale developed and a standardized rubric to assess projects' quality. Each group may wish to revise its report on the basis of the feedback they receive and their response to the reports of the other groups.

8. Students turn in their projects to be assessed by the faculty. An individual test may be given on the content of the project.

9. Teachers may extend the assignment by asking students to apply what they have just learned in a more complex project.

Teacher's Role in Assigning Group Projects

Assigning group projects have three distinct phases:

1. Preparation
2. Monitoring and supervision
3. Assessing the results

Assessment activities take place before, during, and after the project is completed. While not all of the following suggestions for implementing group projects and assessing the quality of students' work will fit every class, consider them carefully while planning group projects for your classes.

Stage 1: Preparation

Preparing Students

Preparing students to work on group projects involves ensuring that they have two sets of competencies. The first is the academic skills they need to complete the project. These should be taught before and during the project. Students should know how to develop the kind of project being assigned.

The second set of competencies is the procedures and skills needed to work together cooperatively. Teachers may wish to explain to students why they will be working in cooperative groups and use a variety of cooperative learning activities to train students in teamwork procedures and skills. Teachers should start with short, in-class group activities (5–10 minutes) and progress to longer ones. They may wish to give every group member a role and rotate those roles to help students learn needed social skills and establishing norms for equal participation and effort by group members. It is helpful to change groups often by counting off randomly so that every student gets to work with every other student in the class. This way, students will learn that they can work with just about everyone and may discover with whom they can really work well. Teachers should avoid letting students choose their own groups, as students may just choose their friends and not look for the potential in others.

Establishing Norms

Establish norms for working cooperatively, and emphasize you will be observing for them. Norms include the following: Everyone participates; everyone explains his or her reasoning processes and what he or she is learning; everyone does his or her fair share of the work; and everyone helps, shares, assists, and encourages each other's efforts to learn. Watch for students who are skillful at working with others and give them positive feedback. Look for those who are not working well in the teams and call them aside and ask them what the problem is; help them learn to be helpful. It is useful to have the class make a Project Teamwork Code. Ask the class, "What are appropriate and inappropriate behaviors in a project team?" Teachers add their own ideas. Making this list helps students think about the norms for project teams and lets students know that you consider their behavior in the group important.

Five Basic Elements: Careful Structuring

Teachers ensure that the five basic elements of cooperative learning are included in the project plan: positive interdependence, individual accountability, promotive interaction, social skills, and group processing.

Teacher's Preinstructional Decisions

Teachers should give some thought to a set of preinstructional decisions (Johnson, Johnson, & Holubec, 1998b). They include deciding on the academic objectives of the project, the size of groups, how students will be assigned to groups, what roles if any will be assigned to students, what materials the groups need, and how the room needs to be arranged. In assigning students to project teams, the safest procedure is random assignment. This tends to maximize the heterogeneity of each group. You may wish to be flexible, however, as some students work long hours after school or have other responsibilities that may limit the time they can spend on meeting after school. Such students should be spread throughout the groups and not concentrated into one or two groups.

Identifying What Students Have Already Mastered

Before the project, a questionnaire may be given to each **student to** identify what he or she knows about the area being studied and the process of completing a group project. The project can then be adapted to ensure that it is academically challenging but not impossible and that the assessment criteria and rubrics can be aimed at a realistic level of achievement.

Planning Formative Assessments

Projects should be planned so that formative assessments can be conducted at regular intervals. Teachers should delineate clear development stages and plan to check the work at intervals along the way. Observations of the groups at work are the primary means of doing so. Groups could be required to hand in progress reports or to do the project in stages, with summary reports after each stage. Individual quizzes could be given to students to see how much they have learned so far or to show their competence at various stages of project development. For example, each student could write and hand in a short paragraph on what their project is about and what they have learned so far. If they are supposed to know how to conduct a literature search in the library, a quiz can be given on how to do so.

Planning for Summative Assessments

The criteria and rubrics used to assess the quality of the finished product should be given to students and clearly understood by them before the project is begun so they know on what basis the project will be assessed and evaluated. Students need to know the standard for success. A set of criteria and rubrics that describe the requirements of the project at varying levels (attributes of an "A" project, a "B" project, on so forth) should be developed—if possible, with student involvement. This takes time to do well, but it pays off with easier assessment and grading at the end. Criteria categories should be arranged in a point system to give more weight to the most critical criteria, and rubrics should be developed in class discussions. The criteria and rubrics define the major aspects of completing the project and should be closely tied in language and sequence to descriptive handouts for the project. This requires defining the process of completing the project. Leeway should be provided, however, for idiosyncratic and serendipitous qualities of completed projects (such as creativity) that were not anticipated when the group project was planned. The criteria and rubrics ideally should fit on one page, with space for comments under each criterion. An example of such a page is given in Figure 5.1.

Stage 2: Monitor and Supervise the Work

No student should ever be able to tell a teacher after a project has been completed that (1) a member did not attend meetings or contribute to the work or (2) their ideas were not listened to and therefore they are not satisfied that the project reflects their best work. By

Category	Possible Points	Points Received	Comments
Executive summary	20		
Problem	10		
Method	10		
Results	20		
Discussion	20		
References, appendix	10		
Organization	10		
[Any points for the following two items?]			
Cover page			
Table of contents			
Total	100		

Figure 5.1   Group Project Evaluation Form
SOURCE: Adapted with permission from Smith (1998).

observing each group as it works, teachers can stay informed and keep the group members on top of problems before they become irreversible.

While students are completing the project, the teacher monitors and supervises the project groups. Teachers do so through such procedures as the following:

1. Observe the groups at work. This is the most useful formative assessment tool. (The procedures for doing so were discussed in Chapter 4.)

2. Interview the groups or individual group members.

3. Collect interim group products and progress reports. Teachers may have the project groups report at regular intervals on their progress. One way to do so is to have the groups keep **group**

folders in which they record each member's work and contributions to the project. Groups turn in their folders at regular intervals to be checked by the teacher. Another way is to have students write one-page (or less) descriptions of how the group is progressing, which allows group members to express reservations or inform the teacher of problems. The teacher can then intervene to help the group solve its problems.

4. Collect informal products, such as one-minute papers (a one-minute opportunity for students to write a response to a particular issue).

5. Have groups process how effectively they are functioning. Each group can engage in its own formative assessments by periodically processing how well members are working together and what progress the group is making in completing a high-quality product. This fosters continuous improvement. Questions might include the following: What are three things you do well? What would make your team even more effective? Are you making good progress toward the goal? Are you maintaining good working relationships? What helps? What concerns do you have?

Stage 3: Assessing Final Products

After the lesson, collect the group products and assess their quality by using the format and rubrics developed before the lesson began. In addition to the group report, the group may be required to present their project to the class. There are several formats for doing so:

1. Each group presents to the entire class (or another class, parents, or other interested audiences). To ensure that all members are individually accountable for knowing the group product, all members of the group may be required to present an equal amount of the group's product.

2. Each group member presents to a set of classmates. Divide the class into new small groups. Members of each project group are assigned to different groups and present their group report to the small group. In this case, each group member has to present the entire report to several other members of the class.

When assessments are used to give students grades, the overall format of the grading decision should be presented to the class. An example is found in Figure 5.2.

Grades Will Be Based on the Following

	Maximum Points
Group	
Group projects (4 at 100 points each)	400
Final examination	
	100
Individual	
Homework assignments (5 at 10 points each)	50
Midquarter examination 1	100
Midquarter examination 2	100
Brief reviews (2 at 25 points each)	50
Heuristics project	75
Review or application project or paper	125
Course grades	
A = 900 points above	
B = Between 800 and 899 points	
C = Between 700 and 799 points	

Figure 5.2   Grade Breakdown in Civil Engineering Course

SOURCE: Adapted with permission from Smith (1998).

Involving Students in Developing Criteria and Rubrics

The criteria and standards of attainment for those criteria (i.e., rubrics) provide guides for qualitative judgments about student work (Johnson & Johnson, 1996, 2002). Teachers and students then know what to look for in assessing the quality of student work and what kind of work represents various levels of attainment, thus increasing the explicitness of standards and the consistency of judgments. While criteria may be specified by national, state, regional, or district norms or by curriculum developers and experts in a field, the rubric under each criteria may be developed by students and the teacher in class discussions. There are six steps in doing so.

The first step in involving students in creating criteria and rubrics is to identify what the performance or product will be and what assessment procedures will be used.

The second step is to develop a set of criteria to use in evaluating the performance or product produced by students. A **criterion** is a predetermined standard used to assess a performance. Involving students in creating what the criteria and rubrics for assessing students' efforts does not mean turning over total control to students. You, the teacher, have a responsibility for ensuring that the criteria critical for the instructional objectives are included. Because you have a clear idea of what some of the criteria should be, however, does not mean that you have to set them all or even most of them. You may wish to reach an agreement with students where you set one-third or one-half of the criteria and they decide on the rest. The steps for involving students in setting criteria are to have them (1) brainstorm a potential list of criteria and (2) rank the criteria from most important to least important. Involve the whole class in deciding what criteria should be used in assessing students' efforts. You, of course, should ensure that the criteria critical for the instructional objectives are included.

The third step is to construct a rubric for each criterion. A **rubric** is a list of indicators of different levels of a criterion, usually a scale ranking from poor to good; rubrics are used to assess the quality and quantity of students' performance for each criterion. Have students construct a rubric for each criterion. Begin with the criterion ranked most important by listing indicators of very poor, poor, middle, good, and very good levels of performance. Once the rubrics are developed, they must be field-tested and refined before they are adopted. Field-testing consists of the two steps of (1) having assessors analyze exemplary and very poor student performances to ensure that each rubric accurately measures the students' strengths and weaknesses and (2) applying each rubric to a set of sample performances to ensure that it works. Once the rubrics have been field-tested, they may be adopted.

The fourth step is to train assessors so that they are co-oriented, consistent, and reliable in their use of the criteria and rubrics. Assessors have to be able to apply the same rubric in the same way at different times. Different assessors have to be able to apply the same rubric in the same way. One procedure for training is to have assessors (1) score a student performance together as a group, discussing where the performance lies on the rubric for each criterion; (2) score a set of student performances separately, with each group member scoring the performances on his or her own and then comparing the scoring to see if team members are using the rubrics in the same way; and (3) have at least two group members score each performance and discuss any differences in their scoring until they agree.

The fifth step is to use the results of the assessment to plan how to improve the instructional program.

The sixth step is to continuously improve the criteria, rubrics, and assessors' skills in using the rubrics to assess the quality and quantity of student learning. Continuous improvement is needed to ensure that the subjective definition of the criteria and rubrics do not drift or change. **Scoring criteria drift** exists when, after assessing numerous performances, the assessor's definition of the criteria (and rubrics) changes or is modified or as a new idiosyncratic rubric is created as the assessor gains more and more experience. There is a need for ongoing training to periodically recalibrate assessors' use of the scoring rubrics; just because assessors achieve a high level of interrater reliability at one time does not mean it will continue forever. Criteria and rubrics can sometimes be improved by enriching them with those of other classes and schools.

In addition to retraining assessors periodically, there is a need for criteria and rubrics to change as the academic year progresses. What is expected of students in September is different from what is expected in January. As students master more and more knowledge and skills, the criteria and rubrics used to assess the quality of their work need to become more demanding and reflect higher standards. See **"Creating Rubrics to Assess Student Learning," "Assessment Rubric A," "Assessment Rubric B,"** and the "Sample Scoring Rubric for Brochures on Vocational Programs."

Class Presentations

When students are required to give class presentations, the task is to prepare and conduct a presentation on an assigned topic (Johnson, Johnson, & Smith, 1998). The cooperative goal is for all members to learn the material being presented and gain experience in making presentations. First, the teacher assigns students to groups of four, gives each group a topic, and requires them to prepare one presentation that each group member can give in its entirety. The presentation should be given within a certain time frame and should be supported with visuals or active participation by the audience (or both). Second, the groups are given time to prepare and rehearse. All group members should be able to give the presentation. Third, the class is divided into four sections (one in each corner of the classroom). One member of each group goes to each section. Each student makes a presentation to his or her section. The audience rates the performance on a reaction form provided by the teacher. Each presentation is evaluated on the basis of the degree to which it was (1) scholarly and informative, (2) interesting, concise, and easy to follow, (3) involving (audience active, not passive), (4) intriguing (audience interested in finding out more on their own), and (5) organized (having introduction, body, conclusion). In addition, the teacher adds criteria uniquely aimed at the purposes of the presentation. At the end of each presentation, one copy of the rating form is given to the teacher and one copy is given to the presenter. The teacher systematically observes part of all presentations. Fourth, the groups meet to evaluate how effectively each member

Creating Rubrics to Assess Student Learning

Step 1: Define the assessment procedure. Indicate on the checklist below the procedures the team will use to assess students' learning.

_____ Quizzes, tests, examinations   _____ Homework, extra credit

_____ Compositions   _____ Other:

_____ Presentations   _____ Other:

_____ Projects, experiments, surveys, historical research

Step 2: Develop a set of criteria to use in evaluating the performance produced by students. The steps for doing so are as follows:

_____ a. Brainstorm a potential list of criteria.

_____ b. Place the criteria in rank order from most important to least important.

Step 3: Construct rubrics. Rubrics are needed to assess the quality and quantity of each student's performance for each criterion. Construct a rubric for each criterion.

_____ a. Begin with the criterion ranked most important.

_____ b. List indicators of very poor, poor, middle, good, and very good levels of performance.

_____ c. Field-test the rubric by applying it to examples of exemplary and very poor student performances to ensure that the rubric accurately measures students' strengths and weaknesses.

_____ d. Field-test the rubric by applying the rubric to a set of sample performances.

(Continued)

(Continued)

Step 4: Train students so they are co-oriented, consistent, and reliable in their use of the criteria and rubrics. Assessors have to be able to apply the same rubric in the same way at different times. Different assessors have to be able to apply the same rubric in the same way. One procedure for training is as follows:

_____a. Score a student performance together as a group, discussing how the performance should be assessed on each criterion.

_____b. Score a set of student performances separately, with each team member scoring the performances on his or her own. Then compare the scoring to see if team members are using the rubrics in the same way.

_____c. Score all student performances with at least two team members scoring each performance. Discuss any differences in the scoring until two or more team members agree on the scoring of each student performance.

Step 5: Plan how to improve the instructional program on the basis of the assessment results. List suggestions:

1.

2.

3.

Step 6: Continually improve the criteria, the rubrics, and the assessors' skills in using the rubrics to assess the quality and quality of student learning. Beware of scoring criteria drift. Remember the need to periodically recalibrate team members' use of the scoring rubrics. Search for exemplary criteria and rubrics other classes and schools are using to improve your classes' assessment practices.

Assessment Rubric A

Student: _____ Date: _____ Class: _____

Type of performance: _____

Write the indicators for each of the five levels of performance for each criterion.

Very Poor	Poor	Middle	Good	Very Good

Criterion 1:
- • • • •
- • • • •
- • • • •

Criterion 2
- • • • •
- • • • •
- • • • •

Criterion 3
- • • • •
- • • • •
- • • • •

Criterion 4
- • • • •
- • • • •
- • • • •

Criterion 5
- • • • •
- • • • •
- • • • •

Comments:

Assessment Rubric B

Student: _____ Date: _____ Class: _____

Type of performance: _____

Write the indicators for each of the levels of performance for each criterion.

Inadequate	Middle	Excellent
Criterion 1		
•	•	•
•	•	•
•	•	•
Criterion 2		
•	•	•
•	•	•
•	•	•
Criterion 3		
•	•	•
•	•	•
•	•	•
Criterion 4		
•	•	•
•	•	•
•	•	•
Criterion 5		
•	•	•
•	•	•
•	•	•

Comments:

Scoring Rubric for Brochures on Vocational Programs

Assignment: Each group selects and researches a vocational program and prepares an instructional brochure to present to the class.

Scoring Rubric

1. Criterion: **Quality of Research**
   1----------2----------3----------4----------5
   One source   Three sources   Five sources

2. Criterion: **Question-and-Answer Section**
   1----------2----------3----------4----------5
   Many factual errors   Some factual errors   No factual errors

3. Criterion: **Graphics**
   1----------2----------3----------4----------5
   No graphics   Good graphics   Dazzling graphics

4. Criterion: **Organization**
   1----------2----------3----------4----------5
   Random   Clear   Overwhelming

5. Criterion: **Oral Presentation**
   1----------2----------3----------4----------5
   Incomprehensible   Clear   Inspiring

Group Grade
Grading score: _____
22 - 25 points = A
18 - 21 points = B
13 - 17 points = C
8 - 12 points = D

Comments:

made the presentation. Remedial help is given to any member who had problems presenting.

Remember, any performance given by a student, whether it is a speech, a musical performance, a science demonstration, a dramatic presentation, or a videotape project, can be assessed and evaluated by peers as well as a teacher.

Group Grades

When groups produce a single product, all members receive the same grade. Some teachers are concerned about the impact, on students' reactions and motivation to learn, of working together on a group product and receiving a group grade.

Many students have some trepidation about the group grading system, especially high-performing students (Bykerk-Kauffman, 1996; Cable & Judge, 1994; DeMatteo, Eby, & Sundstrom, 1998; Hoffman & Rogelberg, 2001; Karau & Williams, 1993). Low-performing students, on the other hand, may have positive expectations toward group grading situations (Hoffman & Rogelberg, 2001).

Before participation in a task involving a group grade, students generally perceive a competitive reward system as fairest, but after the task is completed, a cooperative reward system in which all group members receive the same grade or reward was viewed as the fairest (Deutsch, 1979). Deutsch (1949) found that students preferred the grading system (either individual or group) under which they were currently working.

Once group grades are awarded, they are generally perceived as fair or as neutral. When a group grade has been given, researchers have found that the use of other groups' and teacher's assessments of group performance to be perceived as fair by students (Basu & Middendorf, 1995; Morahan-Martin, 1996) or as neutral: In a survey of business students at a single college, Alexander and Stone (1997) found the assignment of the same grade to all students who had worked on a group project to be perceived as neither fair nor unfair. Hwong, Caswell, Johnson, and Johnson (1993) found that college students studying within cooperative learning groups in which all group members received the same grade perceived the grading system to be fairer than did college students studying individualistically. Wheeler and Ryan (1973) found that students preferred group grades over individual ones. Even when their task performances were markedly discrepant, members of cooperative groups viewed themselves and their groupmates as being similar in overall ability and deservingness of reward (Ames & Felker, 1979; Ames & McKelvie, 1982). Individuals who lose in a competitive situation, on the other hand, commonly perceived the reward system as being unjust and consequently disliked the organization and the person in authority (Johnson & Johnson, 1974; Marwell and Schmidt, 1975).

There is evidence that group grades increase achievement. Wodarski, Hamblin, Buckholdt, and Ferritor (1973) found that group consequences (grades) produced significantly higher performance on math tests and peer tutoring than did individual consequences. The group grade was determined by averaging the four lowest scores in a class of fifteen students. Jensen, Johnson, and Johnson (2002) found that when one member was chosen at random and his or her score was given to all members of the group, subsequent performances on tests given individually significantly increased. This study provides clear evidence that the use of group grades promotes a highly effective learning experience when clear, positive interdependence is structured among group members. Jensen (1996) compared the use of group and individualistic quizzes on students' achievement on an examination. Students who participated in the group quizzes and received the same grade achieved significantly higher on the final examination (taken individually), developed more positive attitudes toward the class and the examination, and met with other members of the class more frequently than did those who took individual quizzes.

Individual Accountability

What children can do together today, they can do alone tomorrow.

Vygotsky

Assessing projects includes both group and individual accountability (Johnson, Johnson, & Holubec, 1998b). Teachers structure **group accountability** by assessing the overall performance of the group and giving the results back to group members to compare to a standard of performance. Criteria for excellence need to be established before the project is assigned, and the quality of the group performance is assessed by comparing the performance to the criteria. A group grade or score results, which every group member shares equally.

A common concern with the use of projects is individual accountability. Teachers worry that some members will be slackers who let others do all the work. Teachers structure **individual accountability** by assessing the performance of each group member and giving the results back to each member to compare to a preset standard of performance. There are a number of ways of doing so:

- **Keep the size of the group small.** The smaller the size of the group, the greater the individual accountability.
- **Observe each group and group member** and recording the frequency with which each member contributes to the group's work. Knowing that the teacher is watching and collecting systematic data increases individual accountability.
- **Assign one student in each group the role of checker of understanding.** The checker asks other group members to explain the reasoning and rationale underlying group decisions and answers.
- **Give random individual oral examinations.** Randomly select individual students to explain answers or present his or her group's work in the presence of the group or to the entire class.
- **Have each student present their group's report.** Require each group to present its product to (1) the class as a whole, another class, or parents (each member has to give an equal amount of the presentation) or (2) a small group made up of members of other project groups, other classes, or parents (each member presents the whole product to a few individuals).
- **Have students teach what they learned to someone else.** Each group member can present the group's product to another group and teach that group what his or her group learned.
- **Have students use what they have learned to solve a different problem.** Each student can be given a problem that can be solved only by applying the knowledge and skills it took to complete the project.
- **Give an individual test to each student.** While students are working on the project, individual quizzes could be given to see how much they have learned so far or to show their competence at various stages of project development. For example, if they are supposed to know how to conduct a literature search in the library, a quiz can be given on how to do so. After the group project is completed, a test on the knowledge and skills they were supposed to learn and use can be given that students take individually. Bonus points can be given if all members of the group pass the test at a certain level (such as 90 percent correct).
- **Structure task assignment around a division of labor.** In a division of labor (task interdependence), the work of each group member must complete part of the project in order for it to be finished. In a unit on swamp water, for example, one member might collect the swamp water, one might make the slide, one might examine it under a microscope, and one might write the report. If one group member did not do his or her job, the whole project would grind to a halt.

- **Structure task assignment around divided resources.** Give each group member (or pairs of members) a part of the resources that are required to complete the project (resource interdependence). Each member must contribute his or her resources or information to the group for the project to be completed. If one member does not contribute his or her resources, the final report will be missing vital information, and it will be clear who did not contribute. If one member has responsibility for Jefferson's life before he was president, one for Jefferson as president, and one for Jefferson's life after he was president, the nature of the final report will reflect how well each member did his or her job. A similar situation is created when each member is taught an area of expertise that is needed to complete the project.
- **Assign each member a different role.** Give each group member a specific responsibility that is required for the group to complete the project (role interdependence).
- **Assign each student a new task whose completion requires the mastery of the previous task** (transfer of learning). Each group member is placed in an individual assessment situation that requires the transfer of what was learned in completing the group project.
- **Assign group folders.** A group folder can be required in which the group keeps a record of each member's work and contributions to the project so far, which is turned in regularly for spot checking.
- **Assign one-minute papers.** At intervals, have each student write and hand in a short paragraph on what their project is about and what they have learned so far. The one-minute paper helps students focus on the central themes of the project and provides feedback to teachers about the success of their teaching.

Instructional Procedures Requiring Group Products

There are many instructional procedures that are specifically aimed at creating group products. The products are then assessed to determine the effectiveness of the group and the members' individual mastery of the material used to create the products. Thus a group may produce a presentation or report that is assessed and the same score given to each group member. It may be followed by a test that each student takes individually and receives an individual score. Examples of such procedures include problem-based learning, the case study method, dramatic productions, group investigation, and academic controversy.

Problem-Based Learning

One of the most widespread uses of group assessment is within problem-based learning. **Problem-based learning** consists of presenting a learning group with a problem (written, simulated, or visual [on videotape]) that represents a situation in which the students will find themselves in their careers (and is thus highly relevant) that gives them a focus for integrating information from many disciplines. The problem is presented in the same way that it could occur in the real world. The problem serves as the initial stimulus and framework for learning and serves as a vehicle for the development of clinical problem-solving skills. In medical schools, for example, students are presented with patient problems they will later face in their medical practice. The objectives of problem-based learning are for students to acquire an integrated knowledge base structured around the cues presented in real career situations, gain clinical problem-solving skills, develop self-directed learning skills, and develop cooperative or team skills.

Cooperative learning groups are the context of student-centered learning focused by the problem presented. Students are expected to work in small learning groups, discussing the problem, comparing information and diagnoses, reviewing what they know, coordinating their search for more information and knowledge, and critically challenging each other's conclusions and analyses.

Problem-based learning is student-centered in that students actively determine what they will learn and in what way. They ask questions, offer possible explanations, and critically appraise evidence. In problem-based learning, students take responsibility for their own learning, identifying what they need to know to better understand and manage the problem on which they are working and determining where they will get that information (books, journals, faculty, online information resources, and so forth). The keys for engaging in problem-based learning units are problem-solving skills, self-directed learning skills, and team or cooperative skills.

In problem-based learning, the teacher's role is specifically defined to be quite different from traditional teaching responsibilities. The teacher or tutor does not give lectures or teach factual information, does not tell students whether they are right or wrong, and does not tell them what they ought to study or read. Rather, the teacher asks students the kinds of questions that they should be asking themselves to better understand and manage the problem.

Last, the assessment in problem-based learning focuses on a group product: the solution to the problem presented by the group as a whole. Typically, each group presents its solution to the entire class. Each learning group is expected to communicate effectively the information they have gathered and the solution they have agreed upon. A written report may accompany the presentation. The teacher may assess the quality of the presentation and the written report. In addition, every class member listening to the presentation may assess its quality and give suggestions for improvement. All group members receive the same grade for the presentation and the written report.

Case Studies

A common way to teach how to apply knowledge to practical situations is the case study method. When students can solve one applied problem, the assumption is that solving others will become easier. The case study method has a long and respected research and teaching history in all the sciences. Significant advances in theory and knowledge have come from the thorough examination of a single case. Cases can serve as the catalyst for in-depth and enriched discussions. They have been important sources of teaching material in the legal and business professions for a very long time and are increasingly becoming popular teaching sources in other disciplines.

Case studies are used for instructional purposes in two ways. First, an actual, ongoing social situation, individual, group, or organization may be examined and analyzed for problems and then an intervention planned as a group project. The procedures for studying an ongoing group may include observing the group in action, interviewing members, examining what journalists and others have written about the group, examining biographical information about group members, and so forth. This information is summarized, analyzed, and used to construct an overall picture, plan an intervention to solve the identified problems, and improve the effectiveness with which the entity is functioning. Case studies have been done on cults, clubs, government leaders at summit meetings, religious communes, rock-and-roll bands, families coping with an alcoholic member or a member with AIDS, and adolescent cliques in high schools.

Second, information about a real or hypothetical problem occurring in an individual, group, organization, or social situation may be given to a group that is then asked to identify the problem and plan a solution. The case may consist of a description of the context, an event that took place in the group or organization, participants' comments (obtained in interviews) about the event, outsiders' observations, and critical commentaries about the event. Discussion questions and possible answers are then given. The format for completing a project based on a case study is as follows:

1. The group reads the case and discusses it until every member understands who is involved and what has taken place.

2. The group discusses and writes down answers to the initial questions. Their answers may or may not be compared with the answers of other groups and any discrepancies discussed.

3. The group reads the participants' comments and discusses them until every member understands who perceives what.

4. The group discusses and writes down answers to a second set of discussion questions. Again, it may be helpful to compare their answers with those of other groups.

5. The group reads the case commentaries by various outsiders and discusses them until every member understands who perceives what and under what circumstances.

6. The group discusses and writes down answers to a third set of discussion questions. They compare their answers with those of other groups.

7. An overall report is prepared on the case to be presented to the class and submitted to the teacher.

8. The criteria and rubrics established to assess the quality of the report is applied to the group's work. Differences among the groups' reports are explored. Each group discusses how well it functioned and how it could be even more effective next time.

Assessing the Quality of a Dramatic Production

In many classes, students are assigned to groups and required to present a dramatic production, such as a play or a video. In assessing the quality of a dramatic production, there are at least five categories that may be assessed:

1. Acting: Did everyone know their lines, did they get into their roles, were their performances believable or truthful, did they make brave or interesting choices as to how to portray their characters, did they use their voices well (they could be heard, words were understandable), did they use their bodies well (gestures could be seen but were not overpowering, movements were understandable, movements communicated what was intended, movements were believable [looked like the character or a normal person], body use was creative)?

2. Direction: Was the overall flow of the production good; did the story make sense; was the story told in an exciting way; were exciting, brave, creative, interesting choices made by the director?

Form for Assessing the Quality of Dramatic Productions

Criteria	Points	Comments
Acting	20	
Direction	20	
Design	20	
Writing	20	
Overall effect	20	
Total	100	

3. Design: Were the set, lights, music, and costumes such that you could see and hear everything you needed to see and hear, and was the right atmosphere and perspective created?

4. Writing (if the students wrote the script): Did the story make sense, were the central concepts and ideas communicated clearly and creatively, were the characters well-developed?

5. Overall effect: How well did the acting, direction, writing, and design work together to create the overall desired effect? (See "Form for Assessing the Quality of Dramatic Productions.")

Sharan and Sharan: Group Investigation

The following procedure is an adaptation of group investigation, which was developed by Shlomo and Yael Sharan and Rachel Hertz-Lazarowitz (Sharan & Hertz-Lazarowitz, 1981; Sharan & Sharan, 1976). It, in turn, is a refinement of the group project method of John Dewey (1970). Group investigation consists of six steps:

1. The teacher presents the class with a general topic or area of study, such as major figures in the American Revolution. Students do some basic research on the topic and propose various subtopics to be studied, such as the lives of George Washington, Thomas Jefferson, and Benjamin Franklin. Students choose which subtopic interests them the most, and groups of two to six members are formed. The teacher encourages heterogeneity of performance level, gender, and ethnicity within groups.

2. Each group decides how the group will proceed to achieve its assignment. In doing so, the members define what the subtopic is ("What do we study?"), what course of action the group will follow ("How do we study it?"), and the purpose of studying the subtopic

("Why do we study it?"). Members (a) discuss their subtopic, (b) divide it into parts (minitopics), (c) assign each minitopic to a pair of members to investigate, and (d) plan the general research procedures each pair will follow. The group focusing on Thomas Jefferson, for example, may divide his life into childhood, before and during the revolution, and as president and afterwards. A pair of members is assigned to develop a report on each part of Jefferson's life.

3. The pairs within each group investigate their minitopic, carrying out the plans developed in Step 2. Members collect and analyze information, evaluate and integrate diverse ideas and perspectives, and reach conclusions. Social skill training may be provided. The teacher acts as a resource person, providing direction and clarification as needed, and creating a stimulating learning environment. The pairs develop their reports on their minitopics (their segments of Jefferson's life).

4. Each group plans and prepares a report and a presentation on its subtopic, as follows. The work of each pair is integrated into one overall report and presentation. The group divides the responsibilities for the presentation among all group members. Each group member is expected to know all the information in the group's report. In the example being used, each member must know and be able to present all aspects of Jefferson's life. One member is appointed to a class steering committee that coordinates the presentations.

5. Each group makes a presentation or display to communicate its findings on its subtopic to the entire class. Each student in the class is ultimately expected to learn all of the material presented by all the groups. Thus each student is required to know about all of the United States revolutionary war figures studied.

6. Students' mastery of the information may be assessed by the quality of their group report, the quality of their presentation, and a test taken individually on all the group reports and presentations. Their investigative skills may be assessed through teacher observations. (See "Group Investigation Procedure.")

Academic Controversy

Academic controversy exists when one student's ideas, information, conclusions, theories, and opinions are incompatible with those of another, and the two seek to reach agreement (Johnson & Johnson, 1979, 1989, 1995a; Johnson, Johnson, & Johnson, 1976). Controversies are resolved by engaging in what Aristotle called **deliberate discourse** (i.e., the discussion of the advantages and disadvantages of proposed

Group Investigation Procedure

Steps	Group Investigation Procedure
1.	Teacher identifies the topic, students divide the topics into subtopics, and groups are organized around each subtopic.
2.	Members of each group discuss the subtopic and divide it into mini-topics that are investigated by pairs or triads within the group.
3.	Pairs investigate their mini-topic and prepare a report and presentation to the group.
4.	The group integrates the mini-topic reports into an overall report on its subtopic. Members plan a presentation to the class on their subtopic.
5.	Each group presents its final report to the whole class. The subtopics thus become integrated into an understanding of the topic as a whole. Each student is expected to learn the material being presented by every group.
6.	Teacher evaluates the quality of each group's report and presentations. An individual test may be given each student on the overall topic.

actions) aimed at synthesizing novel solutions (**creative problem solving**). In academic controversies, students are required to (1) produce a group report detailing the group members' best reasoned judgment about an issue (group members are to arrive at a consensus, ensure that everyone participates in writing a high-quality report, and present their report to the entire class) and (2) individually take a test on both sides of the issue. The controversy procedure is as follows:

1. **Research, learn, and prepare a position:** The teacher presents a topic to the class. Students are randomly assigned to groups of four, each of which is divided into two pairs. One pair is assigned the pro position and the other pair is assigned to the con position on the topic being studied. Each pair is to prepare the best case possible for its assigned position by doing the following:

   a. **Researching the assigned position and learning all relevant information:** Students are to read the supporting materials and find new information to support their position. The opposing pair is given any information students find that supports its position.
   b. **Organizing the information into a persuasive argument** that contains a thesis statement or claim ("George Washington was

the most effective American President"), the rationale supporting the thesis ("He accomplished a, b, and c"), and a logical conclusion that is the same as the thesis ("Therefore, George Washington was the most effective American President")

c. **Planning how to advocate the assigned position** effectively to ensure that it receives a fair and complete hearing: Make sure both pair members are ready to present the assigned position so persuasively that the opposing participants will comprehend and learn the information and, of course, agree that the position is valid and correct.

2. **Present and advocate the position:** Students present the best case for their assigned position to ensure that it gets a fair and complete hearing. They need to be forceful, persuasive, and convincing in doing so. Ideally, more than one media will be used. Students are to listen carefully to and learn the opposing position, taking notes and asking for clarification of anything they do not understand.

3. **Engage in an Open Discussion in Which There Is Spirited Disagreement:** Students discuss the issue by freely exchanging information and ideas. Students are to (a) argue forcefully and persuasively for their positions (presenting as many facts as they can to support their point of view); (b) critically analyze the evidence and reasoning supporting the opposing position, asking for data to support assertions; (c) refuting the opposing position by pointing out the inadequacies in the information and reasoning; and (d) rebutting attacks on their position and presenting counterarguments. Students are to take careful notes on and thoroughly learn the opposing position. Students are to give the other position a trial by fire while following the specific rules for constructive controversy. Sometimes, a time-out period needs to be provided so students can caucus with their partners and prepare new arguments. The teacher may encourage more spirited arguing, take sides when a pair is in trouble, play devil's advocate, ask one group to observe another group engaging in a spirited argument, and generally stir up the discussion.

4. **Reverse perspectives:** Students reverse perspectives and present the best case for the opposing position. Teachers may wish to have students change chairs. In presenting the opposing position sincerely and forcefully (as if it were their own), students may use their notes and add any new facts they know of. Students should strive to see the issue from both perspectives simultaneously.

5. **Synthesize:** Students are to drop all advocacy and find a synthesis on which all members can agree. Students summarize the best evidence

and reasoning from both sides and integrate it into a joint position that is a new and unique. Students are assigned to do the following:

a. Write a group report on the group's synthesis with the supporting evidence and rationale. All group members sign the report indicating that they agree with it, can explain its content, and consider it ready to be evaluated. Each member must be able to present the report to the entire class.
b. Present the group report to the class as a whole (with each group member taking an equal part of the presentation), or each member of the group may present the group report to a small group of classmates.
c. Take a test on both positions. If all members score above the preset criteria of excellence, each receives five bonus points.
d. Process how well the group functioned and how its performance may be improved during the next controversy. Specific conflict management skills required for constructive controversy may be highlighted.
e. Celebrate the group's success and the hard work of each member to make every step of the controversy procedure effective. (See the "Academic Controversy Procedure" and the "Persuasive Argument Composition Rubric.")

Academic Controversy Procedure

Steps	Academic Controversy Procedure
1.	Students research, learn, and prepare their assigned position on the topic being studied.
2.	Students present and advocate their assigned position and listen carefully to the opposing position.
3.	Students engage in an open discussion where they refute the opposing position, rebut the attacks on their position, continue to advocate their position, and learn the opposing position.
4.	Students reverse perspectives and present the opposing position forcefully.
5.	Students drop all advocacy, synthesize the information, and reach consensus about their best reasoned judgment on the issue.
6.	Students' learning is assessed, and groups process how well they carried out the procedure.

Persuasive Argument Composition Rubric

Name: _____ Date: _____ Grade: _____

Title of Composition: _____

Scoring Scale: Low 1--2--3--4--5 High

Criteria	Score	Weight	Total
Organization: Thesis statement and introduction Rationale presented to support thesis Conclusion logically drawn from rationale Effective transitions		6	(30)
Content: Topic addressed Reasoning clear with valid logic Evidence presented to support key points Creativity evident		8	(40)
Usage: Topic sentence beginning every paragraph Correct subject-verb agreement Correct verb tense Complete sentences (no run-ons, fragments) Mix of simple and complex sentences.		4	(20)
Mechanics: Correct use of punctuation Correct use of capitalization Few or no misspellings		2	(10)
Scale: 93-100=A, 87 - 85-92=B, 77-84=C		20	(100)

Comments:

Summary

On many assignments, groups produce a product that should be assessed. Obviously, group assessment cannot take place without groups. Group assessment involves having students work in small groups to complete a lesson, project, or test while a teacher and/or group members measure the level of performance of the group as a whole. A project is an assignment aimed at having students produce a product on a topic related to the curriculum. Projects allow students to be creative and inventive in integrating diverse knowledge and skills, use diverse medias, use procedures such as the scientific method, formulate their own questions and answers, share their learning and accomplishments with others, and transfer and apply a wide variety of diverse information and skills. Projects are usually conducted by groups. When students are placed in groups to complete a project, both group and individual level assessments need to be conducted. There are many desired outcomes of schools that can only be assessed if students work in groups and are assessed at a group level, such as performing a play, winning a basketball or volleyball game, presenting a play, or the making a video. Science experiments, dramatic or musical productions, team sports, history field projects and many, many more assignments may result in a group product that is assessed as a whole. In addition, there are instructional procedures that require group products, such as problem-based learning, the case study method, dramatic productions, group investigation, and academic controversy. In many of these procedures, individual outcomes may be assessed as well as the quality of the group product.

CHAPTER 6

Incorporating Peer Assessment in Groups

Importance of Peer Assessment

Picasso and Braque had an intense creative collaboration, which resulted in the birth of Cubism. They dressed alike, in mechanics' clothes, and jokingly compared themselves to the Wright brothers (Picasso called Braque "Wilbur" and Braque called Picasso "Orville"). For several years, they saw each other almost every day, talked constantly about their revolutionary new style, and painted as similarly as possible. They would have intense discussions about what they planned to paint, then spend all day painting separately. Each evening, they would rush to the other's apartment to view what the other had done, which they proceeded to criticize intensely. A painting was not finished until both said it was finished. Braque later described their creative interdependence as that of "two mountaineers roped together."

> *Almost every evening, either I went to Braque's studio or Braque came to mine. Each of us had to see what the other had done during the day. We criticized each other's work. A canvas wasn't finished unless both of us felt it was.*
>
> Pablo Picasso (in a letter to Françoise Gilot)

> *The things Picasso and I said to one another during those years will never be said again, and even if they were, no one would understand them anymore. It was like being roped together on a mountain.*
>
> Georges Braque

As Picasso and Braque did, students need to assess their classmates and be assessed by them. Peers have powerful influences on achievement-oriented behavior, and there are many advantages to using peer assessment. To be effective, peer assessments need to take place in cooperative (not competitive or individualistic) learning activities. Writing and presenting are two areas in which peer assessments are useful. Assessing social skills requires that students work in cooperative groups and observe each other's actions. All of these issues are covered in this chapter.

Peer Assessment and Feedback

When students work in cooperative learning groups, they become deeply involved in each other's learning. They continuously monitor each other's behavior, become committed to each other's learning and well-being, help and assist each other to learn, and discuss how each member is contributing to the successful completion of assignments. They gain insights into the each other's efforts to achieve, areas of expertise or deficit, and strengths and weaknesses. Fellow group members are in a unique position to provide helpful and constructive feedback. There is even evidence that individuals have more accurate perceptions of other people's actions than they do of their own (Deming & Epley, 2000). One of the most powerful sources of feedback for students, therefore, is their groupmates. Although assessments can be made by teachers and by the students themselves (i.e., self-assessments), peer assessments may be more complete, accurate, and helpful than feedback from any other source.

Influence of Peers on Achievement

Peers have very powerful influences on students' achievement-oriented behavior and academic aspirations (Hartup, 1976, 1978, 1991; Johnson, 1980; Johnson & Johnson, 1981). Peer acceptance is positively correlated with the use of abilities in achievement situations. Students' achievement is related to the level of achievement of classmates and schoolmates, and students are more likely to aspire to higher education and actually attend college if their best friend plans to go to college. Positive relationships with classmates tend to increase achievement motivation, effort to achieve, academic self-esteem, homework completed, achievement, and retention.

Other Influences of Peers

Peers have many important influences on a student's life (Hartup, 1976, 1978, 1991; Johnson, 1980; Johnson & Johnson, 1981). Isolation from peers is associated with high anxiety, low self-esteem, poor intrapersonal skills, emotional handicaps, and psychological pathology. Rejection by peers is related to disruptive classroom behavior, hostile behavior and negative affect, and negative attitudes toward other students and school. Positive peer relationships, on the other hand, are a key indicator of a number of desired outcomes:

- Future psychological health and autonomy (poor peer relationships in elementary school predicts psychological disturbance in high school, and poor peer relationships in both elementary and high school predict adult psychological pathology)
- The acquisition of social competencies, social roles, and social sensitivity (constructive interaction with peers increases children's social skills and social isolation is related to a lack of social competencies)
- Developing prosocial values, attitudes, perspectives, and goals and a predisposition to engage in prosocial rather than antisocial behavior (whether or not adolescents engage in the use of illegal drugs or engage in other problem or possible transition behaviors, such as sexual intercourse and problem drinking, is highly related to perceptions of one's friends as engaging in and being approving of the behaviors)
- Managing aggressive impulses (children learn to master aggressive impulses primarily within the context of peer relations)
- Socializing sex role identity (although gender typing first occurs in interactions between the child and its parents, the peer culture extends and elaborates this process)
- Acquiring perspective-taking abilities (the development of perspective-taking ability and the reduction of egocentrism is largely dependent on interaction with peers)
- Promoting a positive, coherent and integrated personal identity, and creating long-term coalitions that will provide help and assistance in adult life.

Thus having friends who value appropriate social goals (such as educational attainment, a productive career, and self-sufficiency), discourage antisocial conduct, and behave in competent and effective ways gives most children, adolescents, and young adults a developmental advantage. On the other hand, being isolated from peers is one of the major signals of psychological distress and maladjustment.

Advantages of Using Peers in Assessment

There are a number of advantages to involving students in assessing each other's work. First, having students conduct assessments of each other's work provides students with powerful learning experiences that increase their achievement. When students conduct assessments of classmates' work, they learn the criteria and rubrics used in assessment more thoroughly, thus developing internal guidelines and a greater understanding of how their work should be completed. By assessing others' work, students often gain more insight into how to improve their own work than they do from receiving feedback from others. The process of peer assessment makes the criteria and rubrics more salient and helps students gain insight into the requirements of the assignment. One of the paradoxes of assessment is that students typically learn more from conducting assessments than they do from receiving them. Assessing the accuracy, quantity, and quality of classmates' work tends to make the assessment process an important learning experience. Having students assess classmates' work, therefore, becomes part of the instructional program and results in greater integration of assessment and instruction.

Second, having students conduct assessments of each other's work allows for more frequent assessments to take place, thereby allowing teachers to have students engage in important performances more often. When the teacher is responsible for conducting all the assessments, the number of assessments that may be conducted is limited by the teacher's time. Despite how much a teacher wishes to have students write, for example, if the teacher has to read and assess everything each student writes, the amount of writing the teacher can require is determined by the amount of time available. Having students assess each other's work significantly increases the frequency with which (1) important work (such as writing) can be assigned and (2) assessments can be conducted.

Third, having students conduct assessments of each other's work allows for the assessment of a wider variety of outcomes. Besides subject matter knowledge and expertise, student help allows teachers to assess outcomes that require frequent and continuous monitoring or are too labor intensive for one person to assess (such as reasoning, skills and competencies, attitudes, and work habits). These outcomes may be included in an assessment plan when students are available to help. Students may listen to each other's explanations of how to solve math problems, observe each other's teamwork skills, check each other's homework, assess each other's work habits, and assess many other desired outcomes of instruction. When students work together in a group, many of the internal reasoning and problem-solving activities may become overt in group discussions and thereby open to assessment and improvement by groupmates.

Fourth, having students assess each other's work allows for the use of more sources of information in making assessments: Student involvement makes peer assessments available as well as teacher assessments. Self-, peer, and teacher assessments can then be coordinated and integrated. Students and classmates as well as teachers can be involved in communicating the results of assessments to interested audiences.

Fifth, having students conduct assessments of each other's work allows for the use of more modalities in assessment. In addition to assessing each other's reading and writing, students can observe each other presenting, performing cognitive and social skills, demonstrating higher-level reasoning procedures, using visuals such as graphs and illustrations, and even acting out or role playing aspects of the content being learned.

Sixth, having students assess each other's work reduces the bias inherent in making reading and writing prerequisites for revealing knowledge or engaging in a performance. Students can learn subject matter orally and reveal their understanding of what was learned orally. They may interview each other, read to each other, and explain material to each other. Other students can read questions to a classmate who cannot read or write well and assess the quality of the oral responses.

Seventh, having students assess each other's work reduces the possibility of teacher bias. There are numerous ways that bias may be introduced into teachers' assessments: Characteristics such as neatness of handwriting (Sweedler-Brown, 1992) and teachers' perceptions of students' behavior (Bennett et al., 1993; Hills, 1991) can influence a teacher's judgment of a student's achievement. The more that students assess each other's work, the less the potential there is for teacher bias. See "Using Peers in Assessment."

Eighth, having students assess each other's work creates classmate social support systems for remediation and enrichment activities. The limits on teacher time prevent teachers from continuously monitoring each student's efforts to learn; a teacher, therefore, may assess only a sample of each student's work. In cooperative learning groups, classmates can continuously monitor each other's activities. In addition to encouraging each other to learn, keeping track of each other's level of mastery, and holding each other accountable for learning, group members can provide remediation or enrichment activities to members who need them.

Student Performances and Cooperative Learning

Aesop tells of a man who visited foreign lands and, when he returned to his home, could talk of little except his wonderful adventures during

Using Peers in Assessment

Problem	Solution
Missing the learning opportunities inherent in participating in the assessment process	Experience of conducting assessments teaches content and procedures
Infrequent assessments due to amount of time and effort required to implement the assessment process	Students help manage the assessment process for classmates
Limited number of outcomes assessed: usually only subject matter knowledge and recognition of facts	Student help allows more diverse outcomes to be assessed, such as critical thinking, cognitive and social skills, attitudes, and work habits.
Modalities limited primarily to reading and writing	Expand modalities by having students work in groups where they can be observed, perform cognitive and social skills, demonstrate higher-level reasoning, and so forth.
Sources of information limited to teacher assessments	Student help allows for self and peer assessments as well as teacher assessments.
Assessments biased by making reading and writing a prerequisite for demonstrating knowledge and skill	Students can exchange and reveal knowledge orally and demonstrate skills to each other.
Teacher bias and expectations can affect assessment results	Reduce possibility of teacher bias by having students assess classmates' work.
Students receive assessment results without procedures for remediation and improvement	Classmates can provide students a support system for creating and implementing remediation and improvement plans.
Only individual outcomes can be assessed	Students can work together so group outcomes can be assessed as well as individual outcomes.
Assessing individual students in isolation is incongruent with ideal instructional experiences	Have students work together, assessing each other's work, to make the assessment process congruent with ideal instructional methods.

his travels and the great deeds he had done. One of his feats was an amazing leap he had made in a city called Rhodes. "My leap was so great," he said, "no other person could leap anywhere near that distance! Many people witnessed my leap, and if you go to Rhodes, they will tell you that what I say is true." "No need for witnesses," one of his listeners said, "Imagine this city is Rhodes. Now, show us how far you can jump!"

The moral of this tale is that it is not enough to ask students to describe their skills; students have to demonstrate what they can do in actual performances that others can view and assess. **Student performance** refers to a set of actions students engage in to demonstrate their levels of skill in enacting a procedure or creating a product. Gaining competence and expertise in such performances requires students to engage in four activities. First, students must frequently engage in the performances. The more frequently students write, for example, the better writers they potentially can become. Second, students need to receive immediate and detailed feedback on the quality of their performance. Third, students must observe and analyze the performances of others. To learn how to play baseball, for example, one must watch others play and analyze how they field and bat. To learn how to write well, students must study other people's writing and analyze what is good about it and what could be improved. Fourth, students must assess others' performances and provide them with feedback. Doing so teaches students how to improve their own performances. From assessing their classmates' performances, students increase their understanding of (1) what constitutes a high-quality performance, (2) what actions are required to engage in a high-quality performance, and (3) the criteria and rubrics to be used in assessing their own performances.

Performances must be observed and discussed if they are to be improved. If students write every day, someone has to read their compositions and give critical but helpful feedback. The clear fact is that teachers do not have the time to assess numerous performances daily. The labor-intensive nature of performance assessment means that teachers have to engineer assessment systems that involve others. If a teacher has thirty students in a class, for example, that is thirty compositions to assess each day. If a teacher divides the class into writing pairs, however, each student has one paper to assess each day. The former is unworkable; the latter is doable.

Students can most effectively assess the quality of each other's performances within a cooperative context. In a competitive context, students will be tempted to be overcritical of classmates' work to increase their own chances for getting an A. In an individualistic context, students will be unmotivated to conduct quality assessments of classmates' work because it takes away from the time they can spend on their own work. It is only within a cooperative context, where students benefit from the quality of each other's work, that the conditions facilitate high-quality assessments of classmates' performances. Teachers may assign students to writing pairs, inform students that their goal is to ensure that both members of the pair write a composition that meets certain criteria, and then add that if a student's partner's composition exceeds the preset criteria for excellence, the student will receive five bonus points. This clearly communicates that each student benefits from the hard work of his or her partner and has a stake in ensuring that his or her partner writes well. Cooperative learning groups provide an arena in which performances can be developed, practiced, and perfected.

Cooperative Writing and Editing Pairs

There is a ten-step program for having students write together in cooperative pairs (Johnson, Johnson, & Holubec, 1998b). The teacher monitors the pairs and intervenes to help improve their writing during each step.

Step 1 is creating a partnership. Students are assigned to pairs, say hello to each other, and organize all the materials (pen, paper, topic) they need to complete the writing assignment. They are told to work cooperatively to ensure that both write a high-quality composition. Two scores will be given for each composition, one for the quality of the student's composition and the other based on the total number of errors made by both partners (the number of errors in Student A's composition plus the number of errors in Student B's composition).

Step 2 is outlining the compositions. Within each pair, Student A describes to Student B what he or she is planning to write. Student B listens carefully, probes with a set of questions, and outlines Student A's composition. The written outline is given to Student A. This procedure is then reversed, with Student B describing what he or she is going to write and Student A listening and completing an outline of Student B's composition, which is then given to Student B. Students are responsible for teaching their partners how to make an outline.

Step 3 is researching the topic and collecting helpful materials. This can be done cooperatively or individually. In either case, each student searches for information on his or her topic and keeps an eye out for material useful to his or her partner. Students are responsible for teaching their partners how to use reference materials and the library.

Step 4 is writing the first paragraph (or sentence). Pair members work together to write the first paragraph of each other's composition. They are to make sure there is a clear and coherent beginning to both compositions.

Step 5 is each student writing the composition by him- or herself. Working individually, each student writes the best draft of the assignment that he or she can, meeting the criteria set by the teacher (and perhaps the class).

Step 6 is editing the partner's composition. Pair members trade compositions, carefully read what their partner has written, and make suggestions as to how the partner may improve his or her composition and better meet the preset criteria. When both have finished, they explain their suggestions to their partner and listen carefully to his or her suggested revisions of their composition.

Step 7 is rewriting one's composition (the second draft). Working individually, each pair member carefully considers the suggestions made by his or her partner to improve the composition and decides which ones to use. The composition is revised to improve it and to better meet the preset criteria.

Step 8 is to re-edit the partner's composition. Pair members trade compositions again, carefully read what their partner has written, consider how the partner may improve his or her composition, and make constructive suggestions as to how the composition may be improved, keeping in mind the criteria set by the teacher. When both partners have finished editing, each explains his or her suggestions to the partner and listens carefully to the partner's suggestions. Students keep revising their compositions until both partners agree that each composition meets all the criteria set by the teacher and is ready to be turned in.

Step 9 is signing off. When both partners agree that a student's composition is the best it can be under the circumstances, the author signs his or her name, and the partner signs as the editor who personally guarantees that no errors exist in the composition and the composition is ready to be read by the teacher.

Step 10 is discussing the quality of the partnership (how well did we work together?). Partners discuss the effectiveness of their partnership, list specific actions each did that helped the other to write a good composition, and plan how they could work together even better next time. They thank each other for the help and assistance received and celebrate the success of their partnership. See the "Partnership Processing Form A," "Writing a Persuasive Argument," "Persuasive Argument Composition Rubric," and "Reflection on Peer Editing and Assessment.

Presenting Together

Like all performances, presentations take practice for students to become good at making them. There is never time enough for each student to present to the whole class while the teacher observes. At most, this can happen once a month or so, depending on the size of the class. What there is time for, however, is for each student to present in

Partnership Processing Form

---

1. My actions that helped my partner learn:

   a.

   b.

   c.

2. Actions I could add or improve on to be an even better partner next time:

   a.

   b.

   c.

---

cooperative groups of four (one presenter, three listeners). In this way, each student can present once a week (especially if the presentation is limited to ten or fifteen minutes). While a group member presents, the other three members assess the presentation, and the presenter gets feedback from three other students. The teacher rotates from group to group observing a sample of each presentation and then gives appropriate feedback. There is a ten-step program for having students present in cooperative groups (Johnson, Johnson, & Holubec, 1998b). The teacher monitors the groups and intervenes to help improve the procedures and the presenting.

Step 1 is creating a partnership. Students are assigned to pairs, say hello to each other, and organize all the materials (pen, paper, topic) they need to complete the assignment of preparing and making a presentation. The learning tasks are for students to (1) prepare a presentation, (2) make a presentation, and (3) assess its effectiveness. The presentation has to include visuals, active participation by the audience, or both. The cooperative goal is to ensure that all group members learn the material they study and develop and deliver a high-quality

Writing a Persuasive Argument

Thesis statement (A statement that you want others to agree with and accept but expect others to challenge):

Rationale (The facts, information, and theories gathered that validate the thesis statement, arranged in a logical structure to lead to a conclusion):

Conclusion (a statement that is logically derived from the rationale and is the same as the thesis statement):

Author: _____   **Editor:** _____

Persuasive Argument Composition Rubric

Name: _____ Date: _____ Grade: _____

Title of Composition: _____

Scoring Scale: Low 1--2--3--4--5 High

Criteria	Score	Weight	Total
Organization: Thesis statement and introduction Rationale presented to support thesis Conclusion logically drawn from rationale Effective transitions		6	(30)
Content: Topic addressed Reasoning clear with valid logic Evidence presented to support key points Creativity evident		8	(40)
Usage: Topic sentence beginning every paragraph Correct subject-verb agreement Correct verb tense Complete sentences (no run-ons, fragments) Mix of simple and complex sentences.		4	(20)
Mechanics: Correct use of punctuation Correct use of capitalization Few or no misspellings		2	(10)
Scale: 93 - 100 = A, 87 - 85 - 92 = B, 77-84 = C		20	(100)

Comments:

Reflection on Peer Editing and Assessment

Benefits to Editee	Benefits to Editor
1.	1.
2.	2.
3.	3.
4.	4.
5.	5.
6.	6.
7.	7.
8.	8.
9.	9.
10.	10.

presentation on it. Each student will be given a score for the quality of his or her presentation and bonus points if his or her partner's presentation is given a score above a preset criterion.

Step 2 is selecting a topic. Each person, working individually, selects a topic to present (or accepts one assigned by the teacher) and collects his or her initial thoughts about what he or she may say.

Step 3 is outlining the presentations. Student A describes to Student B what he or she is planning to present. Student B listens carefully, probes with a set of questions, and outlines Student A's presentation. The written outline is given to Student A. This procedure is then reversed, with Student B describing what he or she is going to present and Student A listening, completing an outline of Student B's presentation and giving it to Student B. Students are responsible for teaching their partners how to make an outline.

Step 4 is researching the topic and collecting helpful materials. This can be done cooperatively or individually. In either case, students search for information on their topic and keep an eye out for material useful to their partners. Students are responsible for teaching each other how to use reference materials and the library.

Step 5 is writing the introduction. Pair members work cooperatively to write the introduction for the two presentations. First write the introduction for one of the presentations and then the introduction to the other. Members are to make sure there are clear and coherent introductions to both presentations.

Step 6 is planning the presentation individually. Each student works individually to plan the first version of his or her presentation so that its meets the criteria set by the teacher.

Step 7 is presenting the initial version. Two pairs are combined into a group of four. Each person gives his or her presentation. The other three members assess the presentation (using the criteria and rubrics developed for the assessment) and make suggestions as to how it may be improved. When all four members have finished, students discuss how each may revise his or her presentation and make it better. The teacher rotates throughout the class and samples as many presentations as possible

Step 8 is replanning the presentation (the second version). Things get better the second time around. Students work individually to consider the presentation based on the suggestions made by classmates, decide which ones they want to use, and revise the presentation to improve it so that it better meets the criteria set up by the teacher.

Step 9 is giving the presentation again. Each pair combines with a different pair to form a new group of four. Each member gives his or her presentation. The other three members critically assess the presentation (using the preestablished assessment criteria and rubrics) and consider how the presentation may be improved. The teacher rotates throughout the class and samples the presentations of as many students as he or she can. Each presenter should consider carefully the feedback he or she receives from the other three group members. The teacher may wish to collect the assessment forms completed by the group members to help him or her assess the quality of each student's presentations.

Step 10 is discussing the quality of the partnership (how well did we work together). The partners discuss the effectiveness of their partnership by listing specific actions each did that helped the other to make a high-quality presentation and how each could work together even better next time. They thank each other for the help and assistance received and celebrate the success of your partnership.

Preparation Papers:
Combining Compositions and Presentations

Each week, students write a short paper and present it to their cooperative base group. This assignment compels students to do their

Oral Presentations Rubric

Name: _____ **Date:** _____

Title of Presentation: _____

For each criterion, rate the presentation between 1 (very poor) to 5 (very good).

Criterion	Rating	Comments
Addresses subject, scholarly, informative		
Organized (introduction, body, conclusion)		
Creative reasoning and persuasiveness		
Intriguing (audience wants to find out more)		
Interesting transitions, easy to follow, concise		
Volume, enunciation, eye contact, gestures		
Involving (audience active, not passive)		
Visual aids, props, music		
Other:		
Total		

homework, organize their thoughts, and practice both their writing and their presenting.

1. Students' **tasks** are to (a) write a short paper (one to two pages) on an aspect of the assigned readings and (b) prepare a two-to-three-minute presentation on the paper. Before each class session, students do the following:

    a. Choose a major theory, concept, idea, or person discussed in the assigned reading.

    b. Write a one-to-two-page analysis of it, summarizing the relevant assigned readings and adding pertinent material from another source (book, journal, magazine, newspaper) to enrich the analysis.

    c. Prepare a two-to-three-minute presentation on the paper.

2. Students meet in their cooperative base groups of four members. (As mentioned earlier, the base groups stay the same for the entire semester or year.) Teachers create the cooperative structure by giving the base groups the responsibility of ensuring that each member's writing and presenting continuously improves throughout the semester. Bonus points may be given if all members' compositions and presentations meet the basic requirements for excellence. Students are given (or ideally help develop) a set of criteria with appropriate rubrics to assess the quality of the compositions and presentations.

The base group meets at the beginning of the class session. Students bring a copy of their paper for each member of their base group and a copy for the teacher. Each member hands out the copies of his or her paper and presents a two-to-three-minute summary of the paper to the base group. The other group members assess the quality of the presentation and give suggestions for how it could be improved. Before the next class session, members of the cooperative group read, edit, and criticize the paper. Members then sign each member's paper. The signature means that they have read the paper and have provided feedback to improve their groupmates' writing skills.

3. The cooperative groups summarize what they have learned from members' papers and how it applies to the topic of the lesson.

See "Paper Presentation Assessment Form and "Reflection: My Strengths and Growth Goals."

Peer Assessment of Social Skills

Because group members continuously interact with each other, they are in a unique position to assess each other's social skills on the basis

Paper Preparation Assessment Form

Name: _____ Date: _____

Course: _____ Paper Preparation Number: _____

Rated By: Self/Peer/Instructor/Other: _____

Points Possible	Criteria	Points Earned
10	Has a clear, accurate, descriptive title	
10	Begins with a focus statement	
10	Major terms are defined	
10	Explains why the topic is of interest	
10	Includes analysis and critical thinking	
10	Ends with conclusions	
10	Includes information from two or more sources	
10	Each paragraph begins with a topic sentence	
10	Capitalization, appearance, punctuation, spelling	
10	Other:	
100	**Total**	

Comments, specific suggestions on how to improve paper:

Reflection: My Strengths and Growth Goals

1. The best aspects of my skills in writing are

2. An interesting part of my rationale is

3. Things I learned from editing my partner's writing are

4. My next steps in improving my writing are

5. Aspects of writing in which I could be more skilled are

of their experience in working together. Group members may also be trained as observers who systematically gather data on the actions of each group member. Student observers remove themselves slightly from the group so they are close enough to see and hear the interaction among group members but not taking part themselves in the interaction. Observers do not participate in the academic task or comment while the group is working. Near the end of the class period, the learning group teaches the content of the lesson to the observer. The role of observer rotates so that each group member is an observer an equal amount of time.

There are five steps in using student observers to assess students' social skills (Johnson, Johnson, & Holubec, 1998a, 1998b). The first is to decide what skills to observe. The second step is to teach those skills to students. The third step is monitoring the use of the skills in the cooperative learning groups: Teachers have to know how to construct a structured observation form and how to use student observers. The teacher prepares an observation form and observers use it to determine the frequency with which the social skills are used. The fourth step is for students to analyze the observation and self-assessment data and prepare them for presentation to the group members (such as placing them in bar charts or run charts). The fifth step is giving each member feedback on his or her use of the targeted skills, analyzing the feedback, and reflecting on each group member's level of mastery of the targeted skills. In addition, group members may plan how to improve the quality of the group's work and set goals for improvement. The group then celebrates its hard work and success. See the "Observation Form," the Social Skills Report Form," and the "Work Habits and Personal Development Report Form."

Summary

Peers are the potential source of the most complete, accurate, and helpful assessments and feedback. In addition, peers have powerful influences on achievement-oriented behavior and a wide range of variables affecting cognitive and social development. There are a number of advantages to using peers in assessment, as doing so increases the learning of the assessor; allows for more frequent assessments to take place; allows for the assessment of a wider variety of outcomes and the use of more modalities in assessment, and thereby reduces the bias inherent in making reading and writing prerequisites for assessment; allows for the use of more sources of information; reduces potential teacher bias in assessment; and creates peer social support systems for remediation and enrichment.

Observation Form

Observer: _____ **Date:** _____ **Grade:** _____

Assignment: _____

Directions for use: (1) Put the names of the group members above each column. (2) Put a tally mark in the appropriate box each time a group member contributes. (3) Make notes on the back when interesting things happen that are not captured by the categories. (4) Write down one (or more) positive contribution made by each group member.

Action					Total
Contributes ideas					
Describes feelings					
Encourages participation					
Summarizes, integrates					
Checks for understanding					
Relates new to old learning					
Gives direction to work					
Total					

SOURCE: Adapted from: Johnson, Johnson, and Holubec (1998b).

Social Skills Report Form

Student: _____ **Date:** _____ **Grade:** _____

<u>N</u> = Needs Improvement <u>P</u> = Making Progress <u>S</u> = Satisfactory <u>E</u> = Excellent

Shows Cooperative Attitude (Forming Skills)

_____ Moves into group quietly

_____ Stays with group; no wandering

_____ Uses quiet voice in group work

_____ Takes turns

_____ Uses others' names

_____ Respects rights of others

_____ Positive about working in group

_____ Is willing to help others

_____ Follows directions

_____ Shows courtesy toward others

Leadership (Functioning) Skills

_____ Clarifies goals

_____ Gives direction to group's work

_____ Contributes ideas, opinions

_____ Requests others' ideas, opinions

_____ Summarizes, integrates

_____ Encourages others' participation

_____ Supports; gives recognition, praise

_____ Paraphrases

_____ Facilitates communication

_____ Relieves tension

Facilitates Understanding (Formulating) Skills

_____ Summarizes, integrates

_____ Seeks accuracy (corrects)

_____ Relates new learning to old

_____ Helps group recall knowledge

_____ Checks for understanding

_____ Makes covert reasoning overt

Intellectual Challenge (Fermenting) Skills

_____ Criticizes ideas, not people

_____ Differentiates members' ideas

_____ Integrates members' ideas

_____ Asks for rationale, justification

_____ Extends others' reasoning

_____ Probes, asks complex questions

SOURCE: Adapted from: Johnson, Johnson, and Holubec (1998b).

Work Habits and Personal Development Report Form

Student: _____ **Date:** _____ **Grade:** _____

<u>N</u> = Needs Improvement <u>P</u> = Making Progress <u>S</u> = Satisfactory <u>E</u> = Excellent

	October	February	May	Total
____ Completes work on time				
____ Uses time wisely				
____ Checks work				
____ Welcomes challenges				
____ Listens carefully				
____ Takes risks in learning				
____ Makes effort needed				
____ Meets responsibilities				
____ Strives for high quality work				
____ Appropriately asks for help				
____ Appropriately uses materials				
____ Participates in discussions				
____ Seeks extra credit, extensions				
____ Follows rules				

SOURCE: Adapted from: Johnson, Johnson, and Holubec (1998b).

Peer Assessment of Group Members

On the following scale, assess the other members of your group. Use these criteria: Did the person attend all class meetings, come to class prepared, and contribute to the group's work? Did the person encourage the participation of others? Did the person give help and assistance to others and ask for help and assistance when he or she needed it? Was the person willing to do any work outside of class and bring relevant information back to the group for discussion? Was the person a good listener who respected the opinions of others? Did the person help organize the group's work and make sure everything was done on time?

Very Poor Performance 1—2—3—4—5—6—7 Very Excellent Performance

Group Members	Rating
1. My name is	
2.	
3.	
4.	

Alternative Scale:

1 = C, 2 = C+, 3 = B-, 4 = B, 5 = B+, 6 = A-, 7 = A, 8 = A+

Peers are required if students are to engage in performances such as frequent writing and presenting, have their work assessed, and be given immediate and detailed feedback on the quality of their performances. In addition, to become competent in such areas as writing and presenting, students need to observe, analyze, and assess the performances of others.

For writing assignments, students work in cooperative pairs, are assigned to write compositions, help each other to plan the compositions, ensure that each has adequate material and a good start on his or her composition, writes the composition individually, edits each other's composition, rewrites the composition individually, and then reedits each other's final drafts to ensure that they are ready for the teacher to read.

For presentations, students are assigned to cooperative groups of four, given the assignment to prepare a presentation, help each other outline the presentation, ensure that each has the information needed and a good start, each prepares a presentation individually, each gives the initial presentation to the group, receives feedback on how the presentation could be improved, each revises the presentation individually, and then gives the presentation to another group of students.

One way in which both writing and presenting can be combined is through preparation papers. Students write a short paper on some aspect of their homework each day and give a three-minute presentation on their paper to their cooperative group. The group members assess the quality of the presentation and the paper and give feedback on how each could be improved. See "Peer Assessment of Group Members."

CHAPTER 7

Cultivating Self-Assessment in Groups

Self-Assessment

"No one remains quite what he was when he recognizes himself."

Thomas Mann (1875-1955)

One of the purposes of education is to help individuals better understand themselves. Some of the aims of assessment and evaluation, therefore, are to help students gain insight into what they can do well, what they do and do not understand, the validity of their beliefs and opinions, and the degree of skill they have in various areas. Since **assessment** is collecting information about the quality or quantity of a change in a student, group, teacher, or administrator, **self-assessment** occurs when a person collects information about the quality or quantity of a change in him- or herself. While working in groups, students need to assess their own progress and the progress of their peers.

While all students will engage in self-assessment no matter what a teacher does, there are difficulties in assessing oneself and using the results to guide one's behavior. Many individuals are astute about the shortcomings of their friends, spouses, and children while having no insight into themselves at all. The same people who are coldly clear-eyed about the world around them may have fantasies about themselves. Genuine self-knowledge is rare. Without training, and without the opportunity to compare self-assessments with the assessments of others, self-knowledge may always be inaccurate. It is important, therefore, that students are taught how to make valid and reliable self-assessments, under the guidance of a teacher, while working with others who can provide first-hand, moment-to-moment feedback. Teachers may instruct students in how to engage in productive self-assessments that lead to such outcomes as self-awareness, self-knowledge, a clear identity, and consensual validation of conclusions and opinions.

In this chapter, the importance and benefits of self-assessment are discussed, the two requirements for self-assessment are given (comparison process, gathering relevant information), the procedure for promoting self-assessment is covered, and the use of learning logs and journals to facilitate self-assessment are discussed.

Self-Assessment and Self-Knowledge

Chilon, a Spartan philosopher, after visiting the oracle of Delphi in 556 BCE, wished to leave some of his wisdom as an offering to Apollo in appreciation for the oracle's services. On a column in the antechamber, he carved, "Know thyself." Later, poets told us, "To thine own self be true." Western civilization has taken this advice to heart. Hundreds of books have been written dealing with how to get to know yourself, and the *Oxford English Dictionary* lists more than 100 words that focus on the self, from **self-abasement** to **self-wisdom**. A great deal of effort is expended to increase self-awareness. When your attention is focused on yourself, you are **self-aware**. Focusing your attention on yourself results in self-assessment, which increases your self-awareness, self-knowledge, and self-understanding. See "How Aware Am I?"

Benefits of Self-Awareness

I refuse to be intimidated by reality anymore. . . . Reality is the leading cause of stress amongst those in touch with it. . . . Now, since I put reality on a back burner, my days are jam-packed and fun-filled.

Trudy, the Bag Lady, from
The Search For Intelligent Life In The Universe

Try this experiment: Set your watch to beep every hour, and when it beeps, write down what you are doing and what you are thinking. Do this for seven days. Then count the number of times you were thinking about yourself. Two researchers who conducted such a study found that less than 8 percent of all recorded thoughts were about the self. For the most part, attention was focused on work and other activities.

How Self-Aware Am I?

How self-aware are you? The following questions may help you decide. Rate yourself on a scale from "1" (Disagree) to "5" (Agree). The higher your score, the more self-aware you tend to be.

_____ 1. I am constantly trying to figure myself out.

_____ 2. I am concerned about what other people think of me.

_____ 3. I am always examining my motives.

_____ 4. I often worry about making a good impression.

_____ 5. I am sensitive to changes in my mood.

_____ 6. Whenever I get the chance, I look in a mirror.

_____ 7. I often fantasize about myself.

_____ 8. I am self-conscious about the way I look.

_____   **Overall Total**

_____   **Total, Questions 1, 3, 5, 7 = Private Self-Awareness**

_____   **Total Questions 2, 4, 6, 8 = Public Self-Awareness**

SOURCE: Adapted from Fenigstein, Scheier, and Buss (1975) and Johnson (2003).

When participants were thinking about themselves, they reported feeling relatively unhappy and wished they were doing something else. The truth is, however, that there are many benefits of self-assessment, including the following:

- Self-assessment leads to self-awareness, and the more aware you are of yourself, the more able you are to regulate your actions and behave appropriately in different situations.
- Self-assessment leads to self-monitoring, and the more you monitor yourself, the more appropriately you will present yourself and create the impression you want. **Self-monitoring** is the tendency to regulate your behavior to meet the demands of social situations. It focuses on your ability to interact effectively with different people in different situations. Individuals who are high on self-monitoring tend to be poised, sophisticated, and able to modify their behavior as they move from one situation to another. Low self-monitors are less concerned about the social propriety of their behavior and express themselves in a consistent manner from one situation to the next.
- Self-assessment leads to self-understanding, which enables you to solve personal problems. Psychotherapy, for example, is

aimed to guiding self-assessments to increase self-understanding so you can more effectively solve personal problems, deal with adverse situations, and successfully cope with stress.

- Self-assessment leads to social sensitivity. Self-assessment tends to generalize to the assessment of others and the situations in which you are involved. In paying attention to information about yourself, you also tend to pay attention to information about the situations in which you are in and the other people involved.
- Self-assessment enables you to evaluate your actions against criteria and adjust what you are doing so you will meet the criteria.
- When students assess their performance positively, self-assessment may result in increased self-confidence, the setting of higher goals, and the commitment of more personal resources and effort to accomplishing them. The results may be an increased ownership of learning and a sense of responsibility for one's learning.

Self-assessment is so necessary and central to your life that it affects almost everything people do. There are obvious dangers to lack of self-assessments. As self-assessment declines, individuals attend less to internal standards of conduct, react more to the immediate situation, and are less sensitive to long-term consequences of behavior. Yet despite the necessity and centrality of self-assessment and the multiple problems arising from its lack, there are also some dangers inherent:

- The first danger is that assessment may lead to depression over not living up to your own standards, withdrawal from self-awareness and assessment, withdrawal from the situation, and a continuation of current behavior. The more you engage in self-assessment, the more aware you may be of the discrepancy between your actions and your internal standards. When placed in front of a mirror, for example, many people tend to be uncomfortable. **Self-awareness theory** proposes that the discrepancy between actual and ideal selves can motivate either a change in behavior or an escape from self-awareness.
- The second danger is that self-assessment can result in self-absorption. While self-awareness helps you behave more appropriately and competently, self-absorption results in being so completely focused on oneself that no other cognitive activity can take place. Self-absorbed people are in general more likely to have negative self-images and suffer from alcoholism, depression, anxiety, and other clinical disorders.

Self-Discrepancy Resulting From Self-Assessment

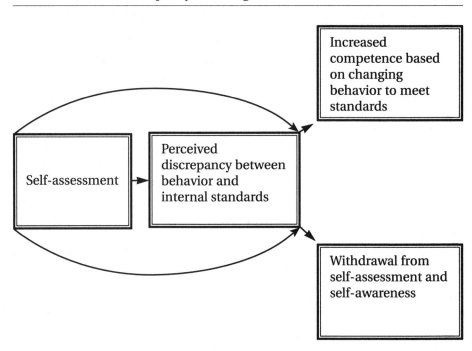

- The third danger is that self-assessment can result in an infinite regression process. **Recursion** is the looping of assessments back on themselves so that information is available to do things over and over until the desired result occurs. Recursion can result in an infinite regression, which is the programming equivalent of those funhouse mirrors that reflect mirrors and mirrors, ever smaller and smaller, stretching away to infinity. Self-assessment and self-reflection may result in something similar. The thought process goes and goes, but it does not get anywhere. Under certain conditions, people can think about themselves indefinitely without changing or understanding themselves better. See "Self-Discrepancy Resulting From Self-Assessment."

Barrier: Inflated Self-Assessments

One barrier to valid and reliable self-assessment is the tendency for people to overrate their abilities (Kruger & Dunning, 1999). People not only overestimate themselves, but they are very certain about their inflated self-judgments, and the least competent performers tend to inflate their abilities the most. The reason for inflated self-assessments seems to be ignorance, not arrogance; inaccurate chronic self-beliefs tend to underlie both overestimations and underestimations of how well a person is doing.

There are a number of reasons why it is difficult to accurately rate one's abilities. First, many areas are subjective enough to allow individuals to bias their assessment toward their strengths and away from their weaknesses. In assessing one's intelligence, for example, there is enough ambiguity in the definition of intelligence that a person talented in math can emphasize math and analytical skills in his or her self-assessment of intelligence while another person may emphasize verbal ability or creativity. Second, in many areas of life, accurate feedback is often nonexistent or ambiguous, making it difficult for individuals to make accurate self-assessments. It is often difficult to get accurate feedback, especially when the feedback is negative. Consequently, it is unlikely that a person will receive criticism that would help him or her improve in performance. Third, people overestimate themselves out of ignorance. Someone can read a book on the stock market and believe he or she is ready to compete with professional stockbrokers. Low performers especially tend to overestimate their performance compared to those who do well. Fourth, many individuals have long-standing views of their talents and abilities that are more related to estimates of how well a person will perform than to actual performance. Thus long-term self-views often result in distortions of perceived performance toward self-enhancement. Dunning and Epley (2000), for example, found that undergraduates consistently overrated the likelihood that they would act in generous or selfless ways and overestimated the degree to which they would act cooperatively. Interestingly, participants' actual behavior was quite close to how they estimated others would behave, demonstrating that a person may see others more accurately than they see themselves.

This self-inflation tends to be more of a Western than a universal phenomenon. Heine (1999) conducted a meta-analysis of seventy studies that examined the degree of self-enhancement of self-criticism in China, Japan, and Korea versus the United States and Canada. In sixty-nine of the seventy studies, significant differences were found between the North American and Asian cultures. In the United States and Canada, individuals tended to inflate self-enhancement, while in China, Japan, and Korea, individuals tended to underestimate their abilities, with an aim toward improving the self and getting along with others. East Asians tended to view a poor performance as an invitation to try harder, while North Americans perceived low performance as a reason to avoid the activity in the future.

Engaging in Self-Assessment

Engaging in self-assessment requires a comparison process and procedures for gathering information about such things as one's performances, actions, emotions, intentions, and values.

Self-Assessment and Comparisons

Self-assessment requires a comparison. Individuals can compare their performance with their own past performances, preset criteria, or the performance of similar others. All three types of comparisons are helpful.

Comparing one's performance with past performances is a very informative way of indicating whether one's competencies are increasing, staying the same, or decreasing. Such self-assessment is especially helpful when performance is placed on a chart or in a graph and recorded over long periods of time. Yet the knowledge that one's competencies are increasing does not give information about the quality or level of one's work. A student can be steadily improving in reading, for example, but still be two years below grade level. For valid and reliable self-assessments to take place, in addition to information about possible improvement in performance, a frame of reference has to be established (either through social comparison or comparison with relevant criteria) that enables the person to make a conclusion concerning the acceptability of the level of performance. Comparison with past performances is informative but does not give information about the acceptability of the level of performance.

Establishing a frame of reference through preset criteria of excellence is a standard procedure in most schools. There is some question, however, as to how relevant criteria get established. Most often, criteria are created on the basis of social comparisons. District and national norms, for example, are established through a normative process as to what percentage of students at a certain grade level performs higher or lower than the student being assessed. The broader the normative group, the more valid the criteria tend to be. Thus national norms are more helpful than district norms, which in turn are more helpful than classroom norms. In a single class, teacher-made tests are rarely designed to give normal distributions, and the class sizes are typically too small to expect a normal distribution (it takes several hundred scores to potentially have a normal distribution). All students with similar training should be included in the norm group. This can be done by (1) incorporating test scores of several sections of the same course taught by the same or different teachers in the same year and (b) using test scores from classes in the same subject taught in different years. The point is that self-assessment requires social comparisons at some level.

A core element of human conduct and experience is interpersonal comparison. One way to answer the questions, "How good am I?" or "How correct am I?" is to compare one's performance and opinions with the performance and opinions of others possessing similar attributes (Festinger, 1954). **Social comparison** consists of comparing oneself with other people in order to make accurate assessments of one's performances, opinions, emotions, attitudes, values, attributes, and abilities. Some comparisons are easy to make. There is little room for error in deciding whether your hair is blond or brunette or how old or tall you are. There are no objective standards, however, for determining how kind, considerate, insightful, intelligent, extroverted, or socially astute a person you are. To make such judgments, you must compare yourself to other people. Assessing your conclusions, intellectual understanding, attitudes, and values requires a comparison with those of others. In the absence of objective measures of evaluation, comparing yourself to others provides a subjective measuring tool. You discover your similarities and uniqueness and form an impression of what you are like. From knowing others, you know yourself. Perceptions of how you compare with others can influence your self-concept, level of aspiration, feelings of well-being, and many other variables. It may be impossible to know yourself without knowing others and comparing yourself with others.

The nature of the social comparison process differs significantly, however, according to whether it occurs in a competitive or cooperative context. In a competitive context, social comparisons tend to be inherently judgmental as to whether one is superior or inferior to others and thereby closely connected with self-esteem and self-evaluation. Winning becomes important, and judgments about self-worth are contingent on whether one wins or loses. There are many reasons why social comparisons have negative results when they take place within a competitive context.

In a cooperative context, social comparisons provide group members with important information about relative achievement they need to help and assist each other improve. Social comparison is also used to gain awareness of the unique combination of qualities each member possesses and the ways in which these qualities may be combined to increase the effort and productivity of each group member. Thus there are reasons why social comparisons will have positive results when they take place in a cooperative context.

Gathering Information for Self-Assessment

Given the multiple benefits of self-knowledge, you need to take Chilon's advice to heart and work to know yourself. There are a number of ways to obtain the information needed for self-assessment. The first way is introspection. You can look inward and examine the inside information that you, and you alone, have about your thoughts, feelings, and motives. Introspection does help you become more aware of who you are and how you are feeling and reacting. Unfortunately, self-scrutiny is not always present, possible, or accurate. Most of us spend very little time thinking about ourselves. The reasons we feel or behave the way we do can be hidden from conscious awareness. In trying to understand our behavior, we sometimes make up reasons for our actions that come to mind easily and seem plausible but are probably incorrect. Introspection is almost always a good idea, but it has its limits.

The second way to engage in self-assessment is to observe yourself. Self-perception theory focuses on this procedure. It states that you understand your attitudes and emotions partly by inferring them from observations of your behavior, the circumstances in which your behavior occurs, or both. By watching what you do, you become aware of what you are like as a person, much as outside observers form judgments of you on the basis of what they see. Often your behavior is a reliable guide to your inner feelings. When you become more self-aware, you usually focus on one facet of yourself. Asking you to look in a mirror physically focuses you on your appearance, while playing a tape recording of yourself speaking focuses you on your voice. When you become aware of some aspect of yourself, you typically evaluate it, considering how this aspect of you measures up to some internal rule or standard. Sometimes you make mistakes about the reasons for your behavior, leading to mistaken conclusions about yourself. You tend to make erroneous conclusions about yourself when

- External influences on your behavior are subtle, and you mistakenly think your behavior reflects your personality: Going to a party with an outgoing extraverted person can cause you to be more outgoing, which you may ascribe to your own personality.
- External influences on your behavior are so conspicuous that you underestimate how much they are influencing your behavior: When a group of friends are all encouraging you to ask someone for a date, you may do so believing that you have decided to do so on your own.
- The causes of your emotional arousal are unclear, so you form mistaken conclusions about what you are feeling: According to the **two-factor theory of emotion**, you first experience physiological arousal and then seek an appropriate label for the feeling. You may not always be right. Some people have misinterpreted being scared as affection for the person they are with (which is why you take your dates on scary rides at the amusement parks).

Your own behavior, however, is usually a useful guide to your thoughts and feelings.

Third, self-assessment takes place when you observe other people. Noting and analyzing other people's actions often result in insights into your own behavior. The more diverse the people you interact with and observe, the greater the potential of achieving insights into yourself. Much of your self-awareness arises from your experiences and interactions with other people. As you get to know others, you get to know yourself. You learn very little about yourself while hiding in a closet and avoiding others. The wider the variety of your experiences with many different people, the better you get to know yourself. By having friends from different cultures and backgrounds, you become more sophisticated about their cultures, and at the same time, you become more aware of your own culture and of who you are as a person.

Fourth, self-assessment takes place when you explain your feelings, perceptions, reactions, and experiences to another person. When you put your feelings and reactions in words, they become clearer, better organized, and take on new meanings. Explaining your reactions and feelings to other people can also lead to new insights into yourself and your experiences. Most types of psychotherapy and many classroom learning procedures are based on the premise that oral explanation results in higher-level reasoning and deeper-level understanding.

Fifth, information for self-assessment is attained when you request feedback from other people as to how they see you and how they react to your behavior. See "Ways of Engaging in Self-Assessment."

Promoting Student Self-Assessment

In every instructional activity, students are supposed to engage in self-assessment. Students are responsible for assessing both the quality of their participation in cooperative learning groups and the quality of their learning. The steps for promoting student self-assessment are as follows (Johnson & Johnson, 1996):

1. Involve students in developing a set of criteria to use in assessing their performances. Criteria should be clearly defined: that is, specific, immediate, and moderately difficult to achieve (characteristics that contribute to greater effort). Students brainstorm a potential list of criteria (each cooperative group comes up with their list) and you (the teacher) add potential criteria to the list. This initiates a negotiation as to what the criteria will be. Neither imposing school goals nor

Ways of Engaging in Self-Assessment

Form a pair. Put in rank order the following ways of increasing self-awareness from most important ("1") to least important ("5").

	Engaging in introspection
	Observing yourself
	Observing others
	Explaining yourself to others
	Seeking feedback from others

acquiescing to student preferences is likely to be as successful as creating a shared set of learning goals that both you and students perceive to be meaningful. Involving students in making decisions about their goals and paths to achieving goals and criteria for assessing progress and success increases their satisfaction and goal commitment. In finalizing the criteria, use student language. Once the criteria are agreed on, the class rank orders the criteria from most important to least important. See "Assessment Criteria."

2. Involve students in creating a rubric for each criterion. Rubrics are needed to assess the quality and quantity of each student's performance for each criterion. Rubrics tend to be three-to-five-point scales. A five-point rubric would include indicators for very poor, poor, middle, good, and very good levels of performance. Students begin with the criterion ranked most important and create the rubric. You find exemplary and very poor student performances and have students analyze them to help develop a set of indicators that accurately measures student performances on each criterion. See "Criteria Ranking Form."

3. Train the students to use the criteria and rubrics so that they are co-oriented, consistent, and reliable. Students have to be able to apply the criteria and rubrics in the same way at different times. Different students have to be able to apply the same criteria and rubrics in the

Assessment Criteria

Rank	Student List	Teacher List	Final Negotiated List

same way. Give learning groups examples of student performances and ask them to decide how the performances should be assessed on each criterion. Have each group member score student performances separately and then compare their scoring with the scoring of their groupmates to ensure that all group members are using the criteria and rubrics in the same way. See the "Scoring Form."

4. Have each student assess his or her performance as you conduct the lesson. It is important that students have guided experiences in how to assess their work against the criteria and rubrics developed. Students are helped to calibrate their assessments by receiving feedback from groupmates (and other classmates and you) on how they would assess the student's performance. When other group members assess each member's performance, self-assessments can be compared with the assessments of groupmates (See "My Checklist for Cooperative Groups."). Thus comparative data is provided from different sources and the differences can be discussed.

5. Help students develop action plans. Have students develop action plans to improve their performance on the basis of their assessments. Students identify their strengths and weaknesses relevant to the lesson, generate improvement goals for learning and self-assessment

Criteria Ranking Form

Very Poor	Poor	Middle	Good	Very Good
Criterion ranked 1				
•	•	•	•	•
•	•	•	•	•
•	•	•	•	•
Criterion ranked 2				
•	•	•	•	•
•	•	•	•	•
•	•	•	•	•
Criterion ranked 3				
•	•	•	•	•
•	•	•	•	•
•	•	•	•	•

Scoring Form

My Scores	Groupmate Scores	Groupmate Scores	Groupmate Scores	Consensus Scores

My Checklist for Cooperative Groups

Name: _____ Date: _____ Class: _____

1. When I knew an answer or had an idea, I shared it with the group.
   Never 1---2---3---4---5 Always

2. When my answer did not agree with someone else's, I tried to find out why.
   Never 1---2---3---4---5 Always

3. When I did not understand something, I asked others to explain.
   Never 1---2---3---4---5 Always

4. When someone else did not understand, I explained it until he or she did.
   Never 1---2---3---4---5 Always

5. I tried to make the people in the group feel appreciated and respected.
   Never 1---2---3---4---5 Always

6. Before I signed my name to our paper, I made sure that I understood everything, agreed with the answers, and was confident that all other members understood the answers.
   Never 1---2---3---4---5 Always

Skill Assessment Table

Action plan for improving skill:	
Strengths in performing skill:	
Weaknesses in performing skill:	
Improvement goal:	
Ways I will assess progress:	

along with new levels of effort, and assess and chart their progress in achieving their goals. The teacher guides students to develop specific action plans toward their goals (viable action plans in which feasible goals are operationalized as a set of specific intended actions), and students' goals and action plans are recorded as a learning contract. See the "Skill Assessment Table."

6. Have the class continuously improve the criteria, the rubrics, and students' skills in assessing the quality and quantity of their

Student Self and Peer Evaluation Form

This form will be used to assess the members of your learning group. Fill one form out for yourself; fill one form out for each member of your group. During the group discussion, give each member the form you have filled out on him or her. Compare the way you rated yourself with the ways your groupmates have rated you. Ask for clarification when your rating differs from the ratings given you by your groupmates. Each member should set a goal for increasing his or her contribution to academic learning of all group members.

Rating Your Self and Groupmates

Person being rated: _____ Date: _____ Group: _____

Write the number of points earned by the group member:

(4 = Excellent, 3 = Good, 2 = Poor, 1 = Inadequate)

_____ On time for class

_____ Arrives prepared for class

_____ Reliably completes all assigned work on time

_____ Work is of high quality

_____ Contributes to groupmates' learning daily

_____ Asks for academic help and assistance when it is needed

_____ Gives careful step-by-step explanations (doesn't just tell answers)

_____ Builds on others' reasoning

_____ Relates what is being learned to previous knowledge

_____ Helps draw a visual representation of what is being learned

_____ Voluntarily extends a project

Self-Assessment Form

Name: _____ Date: _____ Group: _____

Complete this form comparing your self-assessment with the assessment of your groupmates and the teacher. Discuss the results with your group. Ask for clarification when your rating differs from the ratings given you by your groupmates. Set a goal for increasing your contribution to the academic learning of all group members.

Rate yourself on the following scale:

(5 = Excellent, 4 = Proficient, 3 = Adequate, 2 = Limited, 1 = Inadequate)

	Self	Peer	Teacher	Score
1. Take a position, contributes ideas, opinions				
2. Ask for others' positions, ideas, opinions				
3. Use evidence to support a position				
4. Differentiate the positions proposed				
5. Integrate the different positions				
6. Encourage others to participate				
7. Checks for others' understanding				
8. Listen attentively				
9. Contribute energy and enthusiasm				
10. Am considerate of others				
11. Respect work and property of others				
12. Keep personal work tidy and neat				
13. Overall contribution to group effort				
What specific action will you take next time?				

learning. Periodically, students need to recalibrate their use of the criteria and rubrics. See "Student Self- and Peer Evaluation Form" and "Self-Assessment Form."

Self-Assessment and Group Processing

Group members may rate themselves on the following criteria:

1. Using "I" statements, group members rate how often and how well they personally performed the targeted social skills and other expected behaviors.

2. Using "you" statements, group members rate how often and how well each of the other group members performed the targeted social skills and other expected behaviors. The "you" statements give students an opportunity to give other group members feedback about which actions were perceived as helpful or unhelpful.

3. Using "we" statements, group members reach consensus on which actions helped or hurt the group's work. For each rated behavior, the frequencies can be summed and divided by the number of members to derive an average. Or each group member can publicly share his or her answers in a "whip." The group whips through members' answers, one question at a time, by giving each group member thirty seconds to share his or her answer, with no comment allowed from other group members. A third procedure is having each group member name actions he or she performed that helped the group function more effectively and then name one action the member to his or her right (or left) performed that also helped the group.

4. Group members discuss and reflect on their learning experiences, comparing their self-ratings with the ratings they received from groupmates (and the teacher). Such self- and other ratings allow students to see how the quality of their work has evolved. Then the results are used to help analyze how well group members worked together.

Learning Logs and Journals

Two major procedures for self-assessment are learning logs and journals (Johnson & Johnson, 1996, 2002). Having students keep a log or a journal requires them to assess what they are learning, reflect on the results, gain insights into what they are studying, and plan what to do next.

Learning logs and journals are key tools for having students document and reflect on their learning experiences. **Logs** are a self-reporting procedure in which students record short entries concerning the subject matter being studied. Log entries may be reactions to material covered in class and readings, solving mathematics problems, observing a science experiment, outside readings, or homework assignments. A **journal** is a collection of writing and thoughts that have value for the writer about what the writer is learning and its personal relevance. In their journals, students write narrative entries (such as personal observations, feelings, and opinions in response to readings, events, and experiences) concerning what they are studying. Journal entries are usually more descriptive, longer, and freely flowing than logs.

Using Logs and Journals

1. Assign students the task of keeping a journal or a log related to the content of the course. Explain what a journal or log is. Highlight the cooperative goal of ensuring that all group members keep journals or logs that meet the specified criteria.

2. Inform students of the basic mechanics of writing a journal or log: when their entries should start, how often they are to write an entry, how long an entry should be, how often they will share their entries with groupmates and you (the teacher), how the entries will be assessed, and when the final journal or log is due.

3. Have students begin their journals or logs. To help students make entries, structure the first entry in the first class session, and in each subsequent class session, give a prompt, a lead-in, or a procedure for an entry. Examples of daily prompts or lead-ins are given in the following table:

An interesting part is . . .	I want to know more about . . .
I predict . . .	I wonder . . .
Three important ideas are . . .	The ways I helped others learn are . . .
I need to work more on . . .	I am excited about . . .
A connecting idea is . . .	I believe . . .

4. Have students share their journal or log entries with the other members of their cooperative learning groups on a regular basis (e.g., daily, twice a week, once a week).

5. Have students turn in their journals or logs to you periodically for feedback or a grade based on the number of entries and their quality (or both).

6. Have students complete a self-assessment on their journal or log entries based on the predetermined criteria.

Logs and journals may be assessed by specifying the criteria to be used, developing indicators of high, medium, and low performance on each criterion, assigning point values to each criterion, rating a student's log or journal on each of the criteria, and adding the ratings for each criterion together to determine a total score. An example of rating sheet is given in "Sample Measurements for Assessing Entries." Also take a look at the "Reading Log and Problem-Solving Log Forms.

Learning Logs and Informal Cooperative Learning

One of the most useful ways to use learning logs in a class is with informal cooperative learning. Whenever a lecture, demonstration, presentation, guest speaker, film, or video is used, the combination of learning logs and informal cooperative learning will enhance the quality of instruction and ensure high-quality assessment of learning. In this section, this method of informal cooperative learning is explained and the procedure for using informal cooperative learning with learning logs is discussed.

Informal Cooperative Learning

Informal cooperative learning groups are temporary, ad hoc groups that last for only one discussion or one class period. Their purposes are to (1) focus student attention on the material to be learned, (2) set a mood conducive to learning, (3) help organize in advance the material to be covered in a class session, (4) ensure that students cognitively process the material being taught, and (5) provide closure to an instructional session. Informal cooperative learning groups also ensure that misconceptions, incorrect understanding, and gaps in understanding are identified and corrected, and learning experiences are personalized. They may be used at any time but are especially useful during a lecture or direct teaching.

For lecturing to be successful, students must be cognitively active, not passive. The major problem with lecturing has been said to be that the information passes from the notes of the professor to the notes of the student without passing through the mind of either one. During lecturing and direct teaching, the instructional challenge is to ensure that students, not only the faculty, do the intellectual work of conceptualizing and organizing material, explaining it, summarizing it, and integrating it into existing conceptual networks. Students will be more intellectually active the more they do advance organizing, process cognitively what they are learning, and provide closure to lessons.

Sample Measurements for Assessing Entries

Points	Criteria
20	Completeness of entries
10	Entries recorded on time
15	Originality of entries
15	Higher-level reasoning demonstrated
15	Connections made with other subject areas
25	Personal reflection
100	Total

Rating the Quality of Entries

Number of Entries

1	2	3	4	5
No Entries		Few Entries		All Required Entries

Length of Entry

1	2	3	4	5
Less Than 1 Page		1 Page		Several Pages

Depth and Personalization

1	2	3	4	5
Surface, Impersonal		Partial, Personal		Deep, Very Personal

Thoughtfulness

1	2	3	4	5
Response-Only Response		Examples Response		Examples and Reflections

Originality

1	2	3	4	5
Straightforward		Some Metaphor		Images Highly Creative

Score: _____

22 - 25 Points = A

18 - 21 Points = B

13 - 17 Points = C

8 - 12 Points = D

Comments:

Reading Log

Name:

Date:

1. Key ideas:

2. Connections:

3. Questions:

4. Liked best:

Problem-Solving Log

Name: _____

Date: _____ Class: _____

1. My problem is . . .

2. The best way to analyze the problem is . . .

3. Something that is similar to the problem is . . .

4. Three ways to solve the problem are . . .

5. A question I still have about the problem is . . .

6. I need help with . . .

The following procedure will help you plan a lecture that keeps students more actively engaged intellectually. It entails having focused discussions before and after the lecture (i.e., bookends) and interspersing pair discussions throughout the lecture.

1. **Introductory Focused Discussion:** Assign students to pairs. The person seated next to them will do. You may wish to require different seating arrangements each class period so that students will meet and interact with a number of other students in the class. Then give the pairs the cooperative assignment of completing the initial (advance organizing) task. Give them only four or five minutes to do so. The discussion task is to promote advance organizing of what the students know about the topic to be presented and establishing expectations about what the lecture will cover.

2. **Lecture Segment 1:** Deliver the first segment of the lecture. This segment should last from ten to fifteen minutes. This is about the length of time an adult can concentrate on a lecture.

3. **Pair Discussion 1:** Give the students a discussion task focused on the material you have just presented. The discussion must be completed in three or four minutes. Its purpose is to ensure that students are actively thinking about the material being presented. The discussion task may be to (a) give an answer to a question posed by you, (b) give a reaction to the theory, concepts, or information being presented, or (c) relate material to past learning so that it is integrated into existing conceptual frameworks. Discussion pairs use the formulate-explain-listen-create procedure:
    a. Each student formulates his or her answer.
    b. Students explain their answers to their partners.
    c. Students listen carefully to partners' answer.
    d. Pairs create a new answer that is superior to each member's initial formulation through the process of association, building on each other's thoughts, and synthesizing.

4. **Discussion Summaries:** Randomly choose two or three students to give thirty- second summaries of their discussions. It is important that students are randomly called on to share their answers after each discussion task. Such individual accountability ensures that the pairs take the tasks seriously and check each other to ensure that both are prepared to answer.

5. **Lecture Segment 2:** Deliver the second segment of the lecture.

6. **Pair Discussion 2:** Give a discussion task focused on the second part of the lecture.

7. **Repeat** this sequence of lecture segment and pair discussion until the lecture is completed.

8. **Closing Focused Discussion:** Give an ending discussion task to summarize what students have learned from the lecture. Students should have four or five minutes to summarize and discuss the material covered in the lecture. The discussion should result in students integrating what they have just learned into existing conceptual frameworks. The task may also point students toward what the homework will cover or what will be presented in the next class session. This provides closure to the lecture.

Course Learning Log Procedure

Reflective logs can be used very productively with informal cooperative learning (Johnson & Johnson, 1999; Johnson, Johnson, & Holubec, 1998c; Johnson, Johnson, & Smith, 1998). Require that students keep a learning log for the course. They are to bring their logs to every class session. The log entries are completed as follows:

1. **Introductory Focused Discussion:** To prepare students for the class session, have them complete a short initial focused discussion task. Plan your lecture around a series of questions that the lecture answers. Prepare the questions on an overhead transparency or write them on the board so that students can see them. In their pairs, students (a) come to agreement on their initial answers to the questions and record the answers in their learning logs and (b) record in their logs questions they wish to have answered about the topic. Doing so helps students organize in advance what they know about the topic to be studied and establish expectations about what the class session will focus on.

2. **Pair Discussions Interspersed Throughout the Lecture:** Ask students to engage in a three-minute discussion with their partner and write their conclusions in their learning logs. Pairs use the formulate-explain-listen-create procedure. The conclusions students write in their logs enables teachers to track students' reasoning and identify which parts of the material covered were and were not comprehended.

3. **Closing Focused Discussion:** Ask students to engage in a five-minute discussion with their partners and write in their learning logs

(a) summaries of what they have learned in the class session, (b) how it relates to what was covered in the previous class sessions and the assigned reading, (c) any questions about the material covered today, and (d) how it relates to the material that will be covered in the next class session.

4. **Partners read each other's log sheets** and ensure that they are complete, readable, and reflect what was discussed. They sign their names to verify that they have checked the log entry. See the "Double-Entry Journal" sample.

Double-Entry Journal

Initial Entry	On Reflection	Initials

5. **Students hand in their log sheets**. Read them to assess what the students learned, what the students did not comprehend accurately or completely, and what questions they still have about the material covered.

6. Return the entry sheets the next day and have students place them in their logs.

Summary

Self-assessment occurs when a person collects information about the quality or quantity of a change in him- or herself. Teaching students how to engage in valid and reliable self-assessment has long been a basic aim of education. Self-assessment leads to many benefits, such as self-awareness and self-regulation, self-monitoring and appropriate self-presentation, self-understanding, and social sensitivity. There are obviously disadvantages to engaging in self-assessment. First, doing so can result in discovering that one's actions fall short of one's expectations, which can lead to depression and withdrawal. Second, nonproductive self-assessment can lead to self-absorption, which is an infinite regression process of nonproductive self-reflection. A barrier to valid and reliable self-assessment is the widespread tendency in the Western countries for people to overrate their abilities.

Informal Cooperative Learning Log

Name: _____ Class: _____ Date: _____

Task: Your task is to work with your partner in completing this log entry during the class session. At the end of the session, your partner will check your log page to ensure that it is completed; you will check your partner's. You then hand in your entry for the teacher to read. The teacher will give it back to you tomorrow, and you will add it to your learning log.

1. **Introductory Discussion:** The teacher has presented one to three questions for you to answer. You have five minutes to do so. Work cooperatively with your partner using the formulate-explain-listen-create procedure. Use what you know from the assigned readings and from your general knowledge to answer the questions.

   a. _____

   b. _____

   c. _____

2. **Pair Discussions:** Use the formulate, explain, listen, and create a procedure to answer each question posed by the teacher during the class session.

   a. _____
      My answer: _____
      Your answer: _____
      Our answer: _____

   b. _____
      My answer: _____
      Your answer: _____
      Our answer: _____

   c. _____
      My answer: _____
      Your answer: _____
      Our answer: _____

   d. _____
      My answer: _____
      Your answer: _____
      Our answer: _____

3. **Closing Focused Discussion:** In the space below and on the back of this page (you and your partner have five minutes):

   a. Summarize what you have learned during the class session.

   b. Relate your new learning with what the previous class sessions and the assigned reading have covered.

   c. List any questions you still have about the material covered today.

   d. Predict what will be covered next.

Read and Verified by _____

Useful self-assessment requires procedures for gathering information about such things as one's performances, actions, emotions, intentions, and values. Self-assessment also requires comparison, either with a person's past performances, preset criteria, or the performance of similar others. All three types of comparisons are helpful. Comparison with past performances is informative but does not give information about the acceptability of the level of performance. Comparing one's performance with preset criteria of excellence is a helpful, widespread practice, but to establish challenging and realistic criteria, normative information about the performance of similar others (i.e., district, state, or national norms) is necessary. Social comparison is a core element of human conduct and is used continuously to make accurate assessments of one's performance, opinion, emotions, attitudes, values, attributes, and abilities. It may be impossible to know oneself without knowing others and comparing oneself with others. It makes considerable difference, however, whether social comparison takes place in a competitive or a cooperative context. In a competitive context, social comparisons deal with winning and losing and contingent self-esteem. In a cooperative context, social comparisons lead to a view of each group member as a unique individual and to gathering information about who needs help and assistance. The ways in which a person gains information to use in self-assessment include introspection, self-observation, observation of others (especially diverse others of similar age and training), explaining oneself to others, and receiving feedback from others.

Student self-assessment is promoted by (1) involving students in developing a set of criteria to use in assessing their performances, (2) involving students in creating a rubric for each criterion, (3) training students to use the criteria and rubrics, (4) having each student assess his or her performance, (5) helping students develop action plans, and (6) continuously improving the process. An alternative procedure is to have students make "I" statements about performance, "you" statements about other group members, "we" statements about the group as a whole, and overall group processing.

Learning logs and journals are key tools for having students document and then assess and reflect on their learning. In logs, students record short entries about what they are studying, and in journals, they record longer narratives about what they are studying. Doing so helps students keep track of what they have completed, respond to questions posed by the teacher, identify problems to be solved, and apply what they are learning to their own personal lives. To teach students how to write useful entries, teachers should show students models of completed journals and logs that range from excellent to poor, give them specific criteria to assess entries, and periodically give them prompts as to what they should write. Entries are assessed against criteria, which may be given different weights. Keeping logs or journals may increase students' awareness of the assumptions they make about what actions are needed to achieve a desired consequence in a given situation. Journals and logs can also be used with informal cooperative learning: Pairs of students write entries before, during, and after lessons. Keeping a log or journal helps students rate the quality of the learning of themselves and their groupmates.

CHAPTER 8

Designing Group
Experiences for Assessment

Collaboration operates through a process in which the successful intellectual achievements of one person arouse the intellectual passions and enthusiasms of others, and through a process in which a fact that was at first expressed by only one individual becomes a common intellectual possession instead of fading away into isolation.

Alexander Humboldt

This chapter will present guidelines and examples for designing group situations for assessment purposes. Group procedures may be specially designed to assess students' competencies and learning. The two main procedures for doing so are role playing and simulations.

Role Playing

One way in which to assess diverse outcomes, such as students' social skills, their ability to apply knowledge in certain situations, and a wide variety of other outcomes, is to place them in role-playing situations and then observe their behavior (Johnson & F. Johnson, 2003). Role playing is a tool for bringing patterns of behavior and their consequences into focus by allowing students to do the following:

1. Concretely experience the situation

2. Identify effective and ineffective behavior

3. Gain insight into their own behaviors

4. Practice the skills required to manage similar situations constructively

Role playing is a vital training tool for mastering new skills. It can simulate real-life situations, making it possible to try new ways of handling them without suffering any serious consequences if the methods fail. Within a role-playing situation an imaginary situation is set up in which individuals act and react in terms of the assumptions they are asked to adopt, the beliefs they are asked to hold, and the characters they are asked to play. The outcome of a role-playing situation is not determined in advance, and the situation is not rehearsed. Initial instructions are given and the actors determine what happens.

Everyone about to take part in a role play for the first time should hear the following directions:

> When participating in a role-playing exercise, remain yourself and act as you would in the situation described. You do not have to be a good actor to play a role. You only need to accept the initial assumptions, beliefs, background, or assigned behaviors and then let your feelings, attitudes, and behavior change as circumstances seem to require. The role-play instructions describe the point of departure and the beginning frame of reference. You and the situation then take over.
>
> Your experiences in participating in the role play may lead you to change your attitudes and future behavior. You may have emotional experiences that were not expected when the role playing began. The more real the role playing and the more effective the exercise, the more emotional involvement you will feel and the more you will learn.
>
> In role playing, questions may be raised that are not answered in your briefing sheet. When this happens, you are free to make up facts or experiences that accord with the circumstances. Do not make up experiences or facts that do not fit the role. In participating in role playing, you should not consult or look at your role instructions. Once they are used to start the action, you should be yourself. When you are a role player, you should not act the way you feel a person described in the instructions should behave. Being a role player, you should act as naturally as possible, given the initial instructions of the role.

In conducting role plays, there are three important points to remember. First, help the students get into the situation and their roles by introducing the scenario in such a way that the players are emotionally involved. Introduce the scene to the role players. Second, always discuss the role play when it is finished: How could the conflict have been prevented? How did the characters feel in the situation? Was it a satisfactory solution? What other solutions might have worked?

Third, be sure to "de-role" after the role playing has ended. Some students will have trouble getting into their roles and other students will have trouble getting out of their roles. Announce clearly that the role play is over and that students should reflect on and analyze the role play, not continue it. Fourth, conduct a processing session in which students reflect on what happened and how to behave more effectively.

Simulations

There are times when you may wish to observe students engaging in a skill or pattern of behavior, but it will take far too much time to wait and observe the behavior occurring naturally. To save time, you create a simulation and observe what the students do. Simulations and games are being used increasingly as training and assessment procedures. Simulations can vary widely in complexity of issues and number of participants, ranging from relatively simple ones for an individual or small group to moderately complex, computerized simulations requiring a number of groups to participate. For assessment purposes, students are placed within a simulation and their actions are monitored and observed so that behavioral measures of outcomes can be obtained. There are four parts to conducting a simulation:

1. **Preparing for the simulation:** Preparations include reviewing the selected simulation's purposes and rules carefully so you can explain them and relate them to your specific instructional objectives. Gather the necessary materials and equipment. Make a time schedule ensuring that you have enough time for debriefing and group processing. Arrange the space.

2. **Introducing the simulation with a warm-up discussion:** The introduction includes the objectives of the session, a schedule of what will happen, a description of the rules, and a description of the specific procedures, competencies, or skills on which the simulation will focus. The expectations for students are explained. The warm-up discussion sets the stage for the simulation, initiates student involvement, and builds a bond among students. The introduction should be brief.

3. **Conducting the simulation:** Assign students to groups, distribute materials, present the scenario of the situation to be simulated, and review the procedure and rules. Keep the simulation running smoothly within the time limits. Systematically observe the groups and collect the relevant data. Remain unobtrusive, observant, and helpful

in facilitating the action. Halt the simulation when the time runs out or when the students reach the point where they are ready for a debriefing discussion.

4. **Having students reflect on what they learned:** After the simulation is completed, the students are asked to conceptualize, analyze, and summarize their experience. They reflect on what they have learned and discover what it all means. This step may be structured through discussion questions or feedback of data about how each person and the group behaved. The personal learning of each participant, their application to his or her life, and the theoretical principles into which the students gained insight as a result of their experience can be focused on. The debriefing may be organized in three ways:

   a. Decide ahead of time the purposes you want to fulfill and plan your debriefing discussion accordingly. Ask the questions that will focus learning on the points you wish to raise and discuss.
   b. Begin debriefing with general questions to determine which aspects of the simulation particularly interested the students.
   c. Ask broad and general questions relevant to several issues raised by the activity.

5. **Summarizing what students have learned:** In a whole-class discussion, students summarize what they learned by participating in the simulation. Ensure that the appropriate theory and cognitive frameworks are integrated into the students' summaries. The emphasis at this point is on integrating appropriate theory and research with their learning experiences.

6. **Applying what is learned:** Have students apply what they have learned and help them relate the skills to their specific life situations. The schedule for the debriefing and the types of questions you might ask are as follows:

   a. Begin debriefing by encouraging students to describe what happened and their personal reactions so that all students know what their groupmates experienced. Ask, "What decisions did you make? What were the results of your decisions? What happened when the activity ended? How did you feel when you did well (poorly)? What made you feel good (bad) during the simulation?"
   b. Analyze the meaning, purposes or benefits of the simulation. Ask, "What do the results mean to you? What key ideas does this experience teach you? What justifications do you have for the

decisions you made? What did you learn about yourself and other group members from the simulation?

c. Analyze the design of the simulation. Compare and contrast the way students behaved in the simulation and how they behave elsewhere. Ask, "In what ways was your behavior similar to your behavior in other parts of your life? How do the various rules of this simulation compare with the rules we follow in other parts of our lives? What does the simulation represent in real life?"

d. Extend the experience by planning future discussions, activities, and simulations that build on the experience. Ask, "If we were to do this simulation again, what would you change? How can we change the simulation to make it closer to real events in our lives? What key ideas from the simulation would you like to pursue in depth? Are there any related activities that you would like to do now?"

e. Summarize the experience to highlight generalizations and conclusions. Summarize what students learned in a way that ties the experience together. Encourage the students and groups to draw conclusions and make generalizations about their experiences. Ask students to list some key ideas from their experiences, make generalizations on the basis of these ideas, and draw conclusions from the generalizations. Ask, "What key ideas, in summary, have you talked about? What generalizations can be drawn from these ideas? From all we have done and said, what conclusions do you draw from this simulation?"

7. **Processing the effectiveness of the learning groups:** Have students process how effectively they worked together and how they might improve their effectiveness and the overall effectiveness of the group in the future. Group processing focuses on social skills and the quality of the teamwork among members.

8. **Assessing the success of the simulation:** An assessment of the success of the session in accomplishing its objectives should be made.

9. **Providing closure:** At the end of the session, a sense of closure needs to be provided by you. This may be achieved by a short, fun, involving experience. Or you may simply say that the training simulation is over.

For a sample simulation exercise, see Winter Survival Simulation: Surviving in a Life-and-Death Situation at the end of this chapter.

Observing and Using Student Observers

In both role playing and simulations, teachers need to observe what students do and give feedback on what students did. Teachers and students need to learn how to observe the process the group is using to achieve its goals. The process includes goal setting, communication, leadership, use of power, decision making, and conflict resolution. Gaining competence in observing involves consciously engaging in formal observation with a wide variety of observation schedules, for hundreds of times, until the observation procedures become internalized and become an automatic habit pattern. Such automaticity is developed by repetition and the use of a variety of procedures.

Observing is aimed at describing and recording behavior as it occurs. From the behavior of group members, an observer can make inferences about the group process—the way in which the group is functioning. The problem with observation of groups is the potential for lack of objectivity by the observers (Hastorf & Cantril, 1954). Each group member is biased in ways that may affect his or her perception and assessment of what is taking place in the group. A solution to the problem of bias is the use of structured coding systems, which require observers to categorize each group behavior into an objectively definable category.

Four steps are usually involved in observation. The first step is, as usual, to prepare. You must decide which member behaviors, actions, and skills are to be observed. Choose a member from each group to be an observer. You should observe all of the groups, and therefore, make a sampling plan (how long you will observe each group, in what order you will observe the groups). Next, find or construct an observation form or checklist that specifies observable and countable behaviors reflecting the aspect of group process to be studied. Sample observation sheets are included in this book, as you will have seen. Train the observers to use the selected or created form. Second, observe and record how often each member performs the specified behaviors. When there is more than one observer, you may be able to focus on only some of the group members. Third, look at the frequency with which group members are engaged in the specified behaviors and then infer how well the group is functioning in that aspect of the group process under observation. The final step is to summarize the observations in a manner that is clear and useful and then present the summary to the group as feedback. The group can then discuss the observations and revise the group process to make it more effective.

You may present your observations to each group or to the class as a whole. Student observers report the results of their observations to the other group members as feedback. **Feedback** is information on actual performance that individuals compare with criteria for ideal performance. When feedback is given skillfully, it generates energy, directs the energy toward constructive action, and transforms the energy into action toward improving the performance of the teamwork skills. Member performance improves, and the discrepancy between actual and real performance decreases. Increased self-efficacy tends to result. Members tend to feel empowered to be even more effective next time. The "Feedback Checklist" given in Chapter 4 may help in assessing the effectiveness of feedback.

The purpose of process observation is to clarify and improve the ways in which the group is presently functioning, through an objective assessment of the interaction among members. Information about group process is collected and then openly discussed so that modifications in group procedures and members' behavior can be made to improve the group's effectiveness.

Over time, you will develop skills in observing group process. At first, the observation tasks specified in the simulations will seem difficult, but you will find them easier and more helpful as your skills develop. As effective future behavior depends on awareness of the nature and consequences of current behavior, there is no substitute for direct observation in skill development and in the facilitation of group effectiveness. Any effective group member must be aware of group process while participating in the group, and it is through observation practice that such skills are developed.

Constructing an Observation Form

Observation forms are used to answer the question, "How often are certain actions or events happening?" **Observation forms** are used to tally and count the number of times a behavior, action, or event is observed in a specified time period. The form has to be designed so that all potential observers can use it (that is, age appropriate). A structured (formal) observation form is created in the following way:

1. Define exactly what behaviors, actions, skills, or events are being observed (such as, "contributes ideas, encourages participation, checks for understanding, gives group direction"). All observers have to be looking for the same thing.

2. Determine the time period during which the data will be collected. One group may be observed for fifty minutes, or each group may be observed for two minutes. Observations may be summarized after one class session or after several class sessions.

3. Enter the actions to be observed in the first column; each action or skill is placed in a separate row, and the final row is reserved for the total of the columns.

4. Make a column for each member of the group, and make a final column to record the total for each row on the form.

5. Make sure all columns are clearly labeled and wide enough to enter data.

Summary

Group experiences may be created for the specific purposes of assessing targeted student competencies. There are two major methods for doing so: role-playing and simulations. Students participate in the role-playing exercise or simulation, reflect on their experience, relate what they learned to the academic material being studied, and evaluate how effectively they performed in the situation. Group experiences are very useful in assessing complex competencies and skills that need to be demonstrated as well as described.

"Which Books to Take" is an example of a simulation and role play. As promised, the "Winter Survival Simulation: Surviving in a Life-and-Death Situation" comes next, along with its accompanying "Winter Survival Situation Sheet." These are followed by a "Leadership Observation Form."

Which Books to Take

Scientists have suddenly discovered that a large comet is going to strike the earth. All life, if not the earth itself, will be destroyed. You and the other member of your pair have been picked to move from Earth to a new planet. The conditions on the new planet will be harsh and difficult. You will be starting life over, trying to develop a farming and technological society at the same time. Because of the limited room in the spaceship, you can only bring one book for the two of you. "*Think carefully*," the captain says. "*You will never return to Earth. You will never be able to get more books from Earth.*"

1. **Work by yourself** to decide which book you personally want to bring. Choose the book you think will be most
   a. Important to save
   b. Helpful to starting a new civilization

2. **Work by yourself** to plan how to convince the other person that the book you have chosen should be taken. Make sure you are clear about
   a. What book you want to take
   b. How you feel about the importance and value of the book and how you would feel if the book were not taken
   c. The reasons for wanting to take the book and for feeling as you do

3. **Meet with your partner.** Only one book can go. Follow the steps of problem-solving negotiations in deciding which book to take to the new planet and why. You cannot take half of one and half of another. You cannot choose by chance (such as flipping a coin). Each member should present the best case for the book he or she has chosen. Each person must be able to explain the reasons why the book was chosen.

Person 1	Person 2
I want	I want
I feel	I feel
My reasons are	My reasons are
My understand of your wants, feelings, and reasons is	My understanding of your wants, feelings, and reasons is
Three plans to solve the problem are	Three plans to solve the problem are
We choose a plan and agree	We choose a plan and agree

SOURCE: Reprinted with permission from Johnson and Johnson (1995a).

Winter Survival Simulation: Surviving in a Life-and-Death Situation

1. In this exercise you will have the opportunity to practice your leadership skills. You need the following:
   a. A group of five members
   b. One-and-one-half hours of time.
   c. Copies of the
      1. Winter Survival Situation Sheet (one per group).
      2. Ranking Form (one per individual).
      3. Observation Sheet (one per group).

2. Form into groups of five members. In each group, one member is to be an observer; the other four members decide which course of action to take in the emergency situation.

3. Read the situation sheet. Your task is to rank items from most important (1) to least important (12) and write out a rationale as to why you ranked the items as you did.

4. While the observers from each group meet for training, each remaining group member, working individualistically, ranks the twelve items from most important (1) to least important (12).

5. Working cooperatively,
   a. Each group comes to consensus as to how the items should be ranked, including the supporting rationale. There should be one ranking and rationale from the group.
   b. When finished, each group member signs the group ranking sheet. The signature indicates that each person can say,
      1. I agree with the group's ranking and rationale.
      2. I can explain the rationale for the group's ranking.
      3. You have my word of honor that all members agree with the ranking and are able to explain the rationale.
   c. While the group works, the observer observes without participating.

6. All group members are individually accountable to understand their group's ranking.
   a. One member of the group will be randomly selected to explain the group's ranking and rationale to the whole class.
   b. Each group member will have to explain the group's ranking and rationale to a member of another group.

(Continued)

(Continued)

7. All group members score their own and their group's ranking:
    a. Compute the absolute difference (ignore plus and minus signs) between your individual ranking and the experts' ranking.
    b. Compute the absolute difference (ignore plus and minus signs) between your group's ranking and the experts' ranking.
    c. A perfect ranking will have a score of zero. The lower your score, the more accurate your ranking.
    d. Criteria for success:

0 – 20	Excellent
21 – 30	Good
31 – 40	Poor
41 +	Terrible

8. While the group works, you and the other members should practice your leadership actions:
    a. Determine what actions are needed to help the group achieve its goals and maintain effective working relationships among members.
    b. Supply the needed actions or ask another member to engage in the actions.

9. If a group has questions or needs assistance, they can and should ask another group for help. The groups are not competing with each other.

10. The observers report the data gathered about the participation of each member. Group members analyze the data to answer two questions:
    a. How effective was my leadership?
    b. How effective was our group as a whole?
    c. How can I and we improve to be even better tomorrow than we were today?
        1. What leadership actions need to be added to improve the group's effectiveness?
        2. What leadership actions do I need to practice to improve my effectiveness?

Winter Survival Situation Sheet

You have just crash-landed in the woods of northern Minnesota and southern Manitoba. It is 11:32 a.m. in mid-January. The light plane in which you were traveling crashed on a lake. The pilot and copilot were killed. Shortly after the crash the plane sank completely into the lake with the pilot's and copilot's bodies inside. None of you is seriously injured and you are all dry.

The crash came suddenly, before the pilot had time to radio for help or inform anyone of your position. Since your pilot was trying to avoid a storm, you know the plane was considerably off course. The pilot announced shortly before the crash that you were twenty miles northwest of a small town that is the nearest know habitation.

You are in a wilderness area made up of thick woods broken by many lakes and streams. The snow depth varies from above the ankles in windswept areas to knee-deep where it has drifted. The last weather report indicated that the temperature would reach minus 25 degrees Fahrenheit in the daytime and minus 40 at night. There is plenty of dead wood and twigs in the immediate area. You are dressed in winter clothing appropriate for city wear—suits, pantsuits, street shoes, and overcoats. The number of passengers is the same as the number of people in your group. The group has agreed to stick together.

While escaping from the plane, the several members of your group salvaged twelve items. **Your task is to rank these items according to their importance to your survival**, starting with 1 for the most important item and ending with 12 for the least important one.

(Continued)

(Continued)

Winter Survival Ranking Sheet

1	2	3	4	2 - 4	3 - 4
Item	Your Ranking	Group Ranking	Experts' Ranking	Individual Difference Scores	Group Difference Scores
Ball of steel wool					
Newspapers (one per person)					
Compass					
Hand ax					
Cigarette lighter (without fluid)					
Loaded .45-caliber pistol					
Sectional air map made of plastic					
20 By 20 piece of heavy duty canvas					
Extra shirt and pants for each survivor					
Can of shortening					
Quart of 100-proof whiskey					
Family-size chocolate bar (one per person)					
Total					

Leadership Observation Form

Task Actions					Total
Information and opinion giver					
Direction and role definer					
Summarizer					
Information and opinion seeker					
Checker for understanding					
Energizer					
Total					
Maintenance Actions					
Communication facilitator					
Interpersonal problem solver					
Tension reliever					
Supporter and praiser					
Encourager of participation					
Process observer					
Total					
Overall Total					

Directions for Use:

(a) Write the names of a group member above each column.

(b) Put a tally mark in the appropriate box each time a group member contributes.

(c) Make notes on the back when interesting things happen that do not fit in categories.

(d) Write down one (or more) positive contribution made by each group member.

CHAPTER 9

Putting It All Together

Two of the most influential English writers in the twentieth century were J. R. R. Tolkien and C. S. Lewis. While each is recognized by his fans as a genius, what is not always known is that the two men were close friends, deeply involved in each other's work, and they greatly influenced each other's thought and writing (Pearce, 2001).

A clue to how these two disparate individuals become such close friends may be that they were both in a group known as "The Inklings" (which means hint, suggestion, or vague idea.), along with several other writers. The Inklings met twice a week. One of the members would produce a manuscript (a poem, story, or chapter) and begin to read it aloud. This would be followed by other members' criticism and support. Then there might be more reading before the proceedings drifted into a general discussion and often heated debate on almost any subject that happened to arise. This process created a number of important outcomes.

The first outcome was encouragement. In C. S. Lewis, for example, Tolkien found an appreciative and sympathetic audience. "The unpayable debt that I owe to him," Tolkien wrote of Lewis years later, "was not 'influence' as it is ordinarily understood, but sheer encouragement" (Pearce, 2001).

The second outcome was motivation. Tolkien told Walter Hooper that "*I wrote the* Lord of the Rings *to make Lewis a story out of* The Silmarillion" (Pearce, 2001). The meetings of the Inklings represented a network of minds energizing each other into creativity.

The third outcome was pressure to work. In the beginning of 1944, Tokien had done no work on *The Lord of the Rings* for several months. Lewis, noticing his friend's lack of progress, urged him to resume work. "I needed some pressure," wrote Tolkien in a letter, "and shall probably respond." By April, he was writing again (Pearce, 2001).

The fourth outcome was the cross-fertilization of ideas. Through presenting their writings and having them criticized, all members were exposed to each other's ideas and styles of expressing those ideas. Lewis's *Narnia* stories, for example, were deeply influenced by Tolkien's writings (Pearce, 2001).

Intellectual conflict was central to the interaction among the Inklings. Toward the end of the war, for example, in November 1944, Tolkien wrote of a meeting with Lewis and Williams, stating that he could "recollect little of the feat of reason and flow of soul, partly because we all agree so." Later in the same month, in a letter to his son Christopher, Tolkien wrote of

> a great event: An evening "Inklings." In this meeting, Owen Barfield tackled C. S. Lewis, making him define everything and interrupting his most dogmatic pronouncements with subtle distinguo's. The result was a most amusing and highly contentious evening, on which (had an outsider eavesdropped) he would have thought it a meeting of fell enemies hurling deadly insults before drawing their guns (Pearce, 2001).

To create such effective group assessment systems, the misperceptions about group assessment need to be corrected and the eight steps of using groups in assessment must be followed.

Misperceptions About Group Assessment

There are a number of misperceptions about group assessment. The first is that individual assessment requires individual learning. Instead, as we've discussed, learning in a group may increase a student's ability to perform the learned competencies by him- or herself.

The second misperception is that individual assessment measures unassisted learning. All learning is assisted, whether by the curriculum, teachers, parents, siblings, friends, or even the internet. Because groups produce single products, such as a dramatic production, a video, or a survey of the attitudes of local merchants, does not mean that this method of learning is assisted beyond any other form. Having students work in groups tends to level the playing field so that the assistance each individual student receives can be shared with groupmates.

A third misperception is that all learning groups are the same. Nothing could be farther from the truth. There is nothing magical about assigning students to groups and telling them to work together. To be effective, groups must be structured to highlight positive interdependence among group members, individual accountability, promotive interaction, appropriate use of social skills, and group processing.

A fourth misperception is that only the teacher should assess students' work. In actual fact, for high-quality assessments to take place, peer and self-assessments should be even more frequent than teacher assessments.

A fifth misperception is that only the teacher should report the results of assessments. Just as peer and self are powerful and important sources of assessment, classmates need to give each other feedback, and when done skillfully, self-assessments can result in valid and reliable self-feedback. Whoever has the most relevant data should be a source of feedback and the reporting of assessment results.

A sixth misperception is that the assessment data should be collected after the assessment is over. While the teacher can only sample student behavior, when students work in cooperative learning groups, internal, covert cognitive processes may be made overt and open to assessment and correction. In addition, groupmates can continuously monitor each other's learning and provide each other with continuous feedback in order to improve each other's learning.

Another misperception is that instruction and assessment are separate activities. In fact, instruction is considerably enhanced when it is integrated with assessment. When assessment becomes a component of instruction, it provides a systematic review of what is being learned, it can require the integration of what is being learned with previous learning, it can facilitate the creation of conceptual frameworks that provide organization and meaning to what is being learned, it can require higher-level reasoning about what is being learned, it can require a reconceptualization of what is being learned, and it can require students to extend their learning to new situations and problems.

All of these ways of integrating assessment into instruction may be more effective when students are learning in groups and can discuss the results of the assessments with groupmates and then use the results of the assessment in the next phase of the learning activity. See "Common Misperceptions About Group Assessment."

Using the Power of Groups for Assessment

In a single lesson, the teacher may assess the group as a whole and each group member as individuals. Members may assess each other and engage in self-assessment. To tap the power of cooperative learning groups in using and combining the procedures described in this book, the eight steps to using groups in assessment must be employed. Here follows a brief review of the material we've presented in the preceding chapters.

Common Misperceptions About Group Assessment

Misperception 1	Individual assessment requires individual learning.
Misperception 2	Individual learning means unassisted learning.
Misperception 3	All learning groups are the same.
Misperception 4	Only the teacher should assess (peer and self are out).
Misperception 5	Only the teacher should report the results of assessments.
Misperception 6	Data for assessment is collected after instruction is over.
Misperception 7	Instruction and assessment are separate activities.
Misperception 8	Group assessments are uninformative and uninteresting.

Step 1: Recognize the power of groups for assessment purposes

Just as Sandy Koufax's genius depended on Johnny Roseboro, the learning of any one student in the classroom depends on the help, support, and encouragement of classmates. Instruction, learning, assessment, and evaluation all take place in a network of interpersonal relationships. Despite these relationships, assessment has traditionally focused on individual-to-individual transfer of learning and unassisted individual learning, which are reflected in competitive and individualistic learning. Groups have powerful effects on students' behavior, through socialization and development, social influence, and attitude and value development.

The power of groups for both instruction and assessment has been relatively ignored. Students will form groups despite how learning is structured, so the issue is not whether groups will exist in a classroom but rather whether teachers will use the power of groups for instructional and assessment purposes. Learning in groups tends to enhance many instructional outcomes, such as achievement, relationships with classmates, psychological health, and social skills. In addition, learning in groups helps make assessment meaningful, provides the framework for involving students in the assessment process, and enables teachers to conduct more frequent assessments, assess a wider variety of outcomes, use more modalities in assessing students' work, use more sources of information in making assessments, reduce biases in assessment, create support systems, and assess the group interworkings as well as the individual members. Groups mediate the impact of evaluation so that when students working in learning groups have high evaluation apprehension, they perform better on well-learned tasks. But when they have low evaluation apprehension, they perform better on new and complex tasks. Last, a much wider range of outcomes can be assessed when learning groups are used. In short, the use of learning groups opens the classroom to assessment potentials that many schools have not dreamed of.

Step 2: Structure effective (not ineffective) groups

The power of groups reflected in the great achievements in the world and the success of business and industry can also be used in the classroom. As we've mentioned, however, there is nothing magical about working in a group. Some kinds of learning groups facilitate student learning, enhance assessment, and increase the quality of life in the classroom, while other types of learning groups hinder student learning, interfere with assessment, and create disharmony and dissatisfaction with classroom life. To use groups effectively for learning and assessment, teachers must be able to change pseudo and traditional learning groups to cooperative learning groups. There are three types of cooperative learning groups: Formal cooperative learning, informal cooperative learning, and cooperative base groups. The requirements for cooperation include positive interdependence, individual accountability, promotive interaction, appropriate use of social skills, and group processing. Cooperative learning, compared with competitive and individualistic learning, tends to increase achievement and retention, create more positive relationships, and increase psychological health. In addition, cooperation tends to result in more accurate, valid, and reliable perception of students and their performances due to open and honest communication and high levels of trust, while competitive and individualistic learning tend to promote misperceptions of students and their performances based on closed and misleading communication and distrust. To use groups for assessment purposes, the groups have to be structured cooperatively.

Step 3: Make an assessment plan

Louis Faurer's magnificent black and white photographs resulted from his collaboration with his colleague Robert Frank. To gain such productivity in the classrooms, the use of cooperative learning groups needs to be central to the assessment plans constructed by teachers. In making an assessment plan that is then implemented and carried out to fruition, there are at least eight issues that have to be addressed. (1) Teachers may assess individuals, groups, or both. (2) Teachers need to determine the specific processes and outcomes to be assessed; the potential outcomes include knowledge, reasoning processes, skills and competencies, attitudes and values, and work habits. (3) The instructional tasks need to be sequenced. (4) Teachers then formulate the assessment procedures; procedures include tests, observations, portfolios, reports, and so forth. The purpose of assessments may be diagnostic, formative, or summative. (5) The setting in which assessments take place may be artificial or authentic. (6) The stakeholders include students, parents, teachers, administrators, colleges, and employers. (7) The assessment procedures may be criterion-referenced or norm-referenced. (8) The importance of assessment instruction and learning processes, as well as outcomes, is stressed; this is known as total-quality learning.

Step 4: Use groups to assess individual performances

The individual achievements of Watson and Crick in winning a Nobel Prize for their discovery of the double helix resulted primarily from their collaboration. Their assessment of each other's ideas promoted their productivity. Groups can be used for such assessment purposes. The basic purpose of a cooperative group is to make each member a stronger individual in his or her own right. Most assessments begin, therefore, with the teacher assessing the learning of group members as separate individuals. This involves such procedures as setting learning goals, using individual tests and assigning individual products, observing students while the groups work, giving group members questionnaires to complete, and interviewing group members during the group sessions. There is a pattern to classroom life summarized as "learn it in a group, perform it alone." The teacher may use the results of the individual assessments to structure the agenda for the next group session, and the group may use the individual assessments to provide remediation and further instruction of each member.

Step 5: Assess group performances

Kurt Lewin and his students revolutionized the field of psychology through their intense discussion of theories, ideas, and potential research projects. Their discussions were so free flowing that ownership of any one idea could not be established, they were the product of the group as a whole. This is typical of productive groups. There are many instructional procedures that require a group product, and there are many assignments that require groups to produce a single product. Science experiments, dramatic or musical productions, team sports, history field projects and many, many more assignments may result in a group product that is assessed as a whole. Problem-based learning, the case study method, dramatic productions, group investigation, and academic controversy all require group products. Such instructional procedures allow students to be creative and inventive in integrating diverse knowledge and skills, use diverse media, use procedures such as the scientific method, formulate their own questions and answers, share their learning and accomplishments with others, and transfer and apply a wide variety of diverse information and skills. When students are placed in groups to complete a project, both group and individual level assessments need to be conducted.

Step 6: Structure peer assessment

Picasso and Braque's intensely creative collaboration stands as an example of the power of peer assessment. Peers are the potential source of the most complete, accurate, and helpful assessments and feedback. Teachers can only sample student behavior, while peers in learning groups can continuously monitor and assess each other's behavior. Peer monitoring and assessment can have powerful influences on achievement-oriented behavior and a wide range of variables affecting cognitive and social development. Using peers in assessment increases the learning of the assessor, allows for more frequent assessments to take place, allows for the assessment of a wider variety of outcomes, allows for the use of more modalities in assessment, reduces the bias inherent in making reading and writing prerequisites for assessment, allows for the use of more sources of information, reduces potential teacher bias in assessment, and creates peer social support systems for remediation and enrichment. Peers are essential if students are to (1) engage in performances such as writing and presenting frequently, (2) have their work assessed, and (3) be given immediate and detailed feedback on the quality of their performances. In addition, to become competent in such areas as writing and presenting, students need to observe, analyze, and assess the performances of others.

Step 7: Structure self-assessment

The philosopher Chilon wrote in the antechamber of the Oracle of Delphi, "Know Thyself." This is the purpose of much assessment in the classroom, that students develop an understanding of their strengths and weaknesses and areas in which they excel or need further growth. Throughout one's life, learning, growth, and development is greatly influenced by self-assessment. There will not always be a teacher or a set of peers to assess one's actions and provide feedback. Each individual has to learn how to engage in self-assessment and use the results to modify his or her behavior to make it more effective. Teaching students how to engage in valid and reliable self-assessment has long been a basic aim of education. Self-assessment leads self-awareness and self-regulation, self-monitoring and appropriate self-presentation, self-understanding, and social sensitivity. Engaging in self-assessment requires a social comparison process with other individuals. Without comparing oneself with similar others, a person will never really know whether they are quick or slow witted, have a sense of humor, or approach problems in an analytical and rational way. Social comparison is a core element of human conduct and is used continuously to make assessments of one's performances, opinions, emotions, attitudes, values, attributes, and abilities. It may be impossible to know oneself without knowing others and comparing oneself with others. It makes considerable difference, however, whether social comparison takes place in a competitive or a cooperative context. In a competitive context, social comparisons deal with winning and losing and contingent self-esteem. In a cooperative context, social comparisons lead to a view of each group member as a unique individual.

The ways in which a person gains information to use in self-assessment include introspection, self-observation, observation of others (especially diverse others of similar age and training), explaining oneself to others, and receiving feedback from others. Student self-assessment is promoted by (1) involving students in developing a set of criteria to use in assessing their performances, (2) involving students in creating a rubric for each criterion, (3) training students to use the criteria and rubrics, (4) having each student assess his or her performance, (5) helping students develop action plans, and (6) continuously improving the process. Learning logs and journals are key tools for having students document, assess, and reflect on their learning. Keeping a log or journal helps students rate the quality of the learning of themselves and their groupmates.

Step 8: Use groups to create assessment situations

Group experiences may be created for the specific purposes of assessing targeted student competencies and learning. There are two major methods for doing so: role playing and simulations. Students participate in the role-playing exercise or simulation, reflect on their experience, relate what they learned to the academic material being studied, and evaluate how effectively they performed in the situation. Group experiences are very useful in assessing complex competencies and skills that need to be demonstrated as well as described.

Looking Forward

At the end of this book, you may be at a new beginning. Years of experience are needed to gain real expertise in capitalizing on the power of groups for assessment. The groups must be cooperative. They must be central in your assessment plan. They must be used to assess individual students. Group products must be assigned and assessed. Peer assessments must be promoted and used. Self-assessment must be taught and emphasized. Group situations may be constructed for specific assessment needs. It is through groups that assessment becomes a powerful force within instruction and an inherent part of the instructional procedures. Involving students in the assessment process will eventually result in more sophisticated students who can help you continuously improve the teaching and assessment process. The highest level of Bloom's (1976) Taxonomy is generating, holding, and applying a set of internal and external criteria. It is time that much of the responsibility for assessment is shared with students. Working jointly with students creates a learning community in which students' involvement in the assessment process will enhance all aspects of learning and instruction.

References

Alexander, M., & Stone, S. (1997, February). Student perceptions of team work in the classroom: An analysis by gender. *Business Education Forum*, 7-9.

Ames, C., & Felker, D. (1979). An examination of children's attributions and achievement-related evaluations in competitive, cooperative, and individualistic reward structures. *Journal of Educational Psychology, 71*, 413-420.

Ames, C., & McKelvie, S. (1982, April). *Evaluation of students' achievement behavior within cooperative and competitive reward structures.* Paper presented at the annual meeting of the American Educational Research Association, New York.

Astin, A. (1993). Engineering outcomes. *ASEE Prism, 3*(1), 27-30.

Atkinson, J., & Raynor, J. (1974). *Motivation and achievement.* Washington, DC: Winston.

Baron, R. (1986). Distraction/conflict theory: Progress and problems. In L. Berkowitz (Ed.), *Advances in experimental social psychology* (Vol. 19, pp. 1-40). Orlando, FL: Academic Press.

Basu, A., & Middendorf, J. (1995). Discovering new knowledge through collaborative learning in groups. *Journal of Geological Education, 43*, 317-321.

Baumeister, R., & Leary, M. (1995). The need to belong: Desire for interpersonal attachment as a fundamental human motivation. *Psychological Bulletin, 117*, 497-529.

Bennett, R., Gottesman, R., Rock, D., & Cerullo, F. (1993). Influence of behavior perceptions and gender on teachers' judgments of students' academic skill. *Journal of Educational Psychology, 85*, 347-356.

Bennis, W., & Biederman, P. (1997). *Organizing genius: The secrets of creative collaboration.* Reading, MA: Addison-Wesley.

Bloom, B., 1976. *Human characteristics and student learning.* New York: McGraw Hill.

Bykerk-Kauffman, A., (1996). A hands-on approach to teaching the terrane concept in historical geology. *Journal of Geological Education, 37*, 83-89.

Cable, D., & Judge, T. (1994). Pay preferences and job search decisions: A person-organization fit perspective. *Personnel Psychology, 47*, 317-348.

DeMatteo, J., Eby, L., & Sundstrom, E. (1998). Team-based rewards: Current empirical evidence and directions for future research. *Research in Organizational Behavior, 20*, 141-183.

Deutsch, M. (1949). A theory of cooperation and competition. *Human Relations, 2*, 129-152.

Deutsch, M. (1962). Cooperation and trust: Some theoretical notes. In M. Jones (Ed.), *Nebraska Symposium on Motivation*, 275-320. Lincoln: University of Nebraska Press.

Deutsch, M. (1979). Education and distributive justice: Some reflections on grading systems. *American Psychologist, 34*, 391-401.

DeVries, D., & Edwards, K. (1974). Student teams and learning games: Their effects on cross-race and cross-sex interaction. *Journal of Educational Psychology, 66*, 741-749.

Dewey. J. (1970). *Experience and education.* New York: Collier.

Dinan, F. (1995). A team learning method for organic chemistry. *Journal of Chemical Education, 72*, 429-431.

Dysthe, O. (1996). The multivoiced classroom: Interactions of writing and classroom discourse. *Written Communication, 13*, 383-425.

Epley, N., & Dunning, D. (2000). Feeling "holier than thou:" Are self-serving assessments produced by errors in self- or social prediction? *Journal of Personality and Social Psychology, 79*(6), 861-875.

Fenigstein, A., Scheier, M., & Buss, A. (1975). Public and private self-consciousness: Assessment and theory. *Journal of Consulting and Clinical Psychology, 43*, 522-527.

Festinger, L. (1954). A theory of social comparison processes. *Human Relations, 7,* 117-141.

Gardner, W., Pickett, C., & Brewer, M. (2000). Social exclusion and selective memory: How the need to belong influences memory for social events. *Personality and Social Psychology Bulletin, 26*, 486-496.

Hartup, W. (1976). Peer interaction and the behavioral development of the individual child. In E. Schlopler & R. Reichler (Eds.), *Psychopathology and child development.* New York: Plenum.

Hartup, W. W. (1978). Children and their friends. In H. McGurk (Ed.), *Childhood social development.* London: Methuen

Hartup, W. (1991). Having friends, making friends, and keeping friends: Relationships as educational contexts. *Early Report* (Center for Early Education and Development, University of Minnesota), *19,* 1-4.

Hastorf, A., & Cantril, H. (1954). They saw a game. *Journal of Abnormal and Social Psychology, 49*, 129-134.

Heine, S., Lehman, D., Markus, H., & Kitayama, S. (1999). Is there a universal need for positive self-regard? *Psychological Review, 106*(4), 766–794.

Herrington, A., & Curtin, M. (1990). Basic writing: Moving the voices on the margin to the center. *Harvard Educational Review, 60*, 489-496.

Hills, J. (1991). Apathy concerning grading and testing. *Phi Delta Kappan, 72*(2), 540-545.

Hoffman, J., & Rogelberg, S. (2001). All together now? College students' preferred project group grading procedures. *Group Dynamics: Theory, Research, and Practice, 5*(1), 33-40.

Horney, K. (1937). *The neurotic personality of our time.* New York: Norton.

Hwong, N., Caswell, A., Johnson, D. W., & Johnson, R. (1993). Effects of cooperative and individualistic learning on prospective elementary teachers' music achievement and attitudes. *Journal of Social Psychology, 133,* 53-64.

Jackson, J., & Williams, K. (1985). Social loafing on difficult tasks: Working collectively can improve performance. *Journal of Personality and Social Psychology, 49,* 937-942.

Jensen, M. (1996). Cooperative quizzes in the anatomy and physiology laboratory: A description and evaluation. *Advances in Physiology Education, 16*(1), S48-S54.

Jensen, M., Johnson, D. W., & Johnson, R. (2002). Impact of positive interdependence during electronic quizzes on discourse and achievement. *Journal of Educational Research, 95*(3), 161-166.

Johnson, D. W. (1980). Group processes: Influences of student-student interaction on school outcomes. In J. McMillan (Ed.), *The social psychology of school learning* (pp. 123-168). New York: Academic Press.

Johnson, D. W. (1991). *Human relations and your career.* Englewood Cliffs, NJ: Prentice-Hall.

Johnson, D. W. (2003). *Reaching out: Interpersonal effectiveness and self-actualization* (8th ed.). Boston: Allyn & Bacon.

Johnson, D. W., & Johnson, F. (2003). *Joining together: Group theory and group skills* (8th ed.). Englewood Cliffs, NJ: Prentice Hall.

Johnson, D. W., & Johnson, R. (1974). Instructional goal structure: Cooperative, competitive, or individualistic. *Review of Educational Research, 44,* 213-240.

Johnson, D. W., & Johnson, R. (1979). Conflict in the classroom: Controversy and learning. *Review of Educational Research, 49,* 51-70.

Johnson, D. W., & Johnson, R. (1981, January). Student-student interaction: The neglected variable in education. *Educational Researcher, 10,* 5-10.

Johnson, D. W., & Johnson, R. (1989). *Cooperation and competition: Theory and research.* Edina, MN: Interaction.

Johnson, D. W., & Johnson, R. (1994). *Leading the cooperative school* (2nd ed). Edina, MN: Interaction.

Johnson, D. W., & Johnson, R. (1995a). *Creative controversy: Intellectual challenge in the classroom* (3rd ed.). Edina, MN: Interaction.

Johnson, D. W., & Johnson, R. (1995b). *Teaching students to be peacemakers* (3rd ed.). Edina, MN: Interaction Book Company.

Johnson, D. W., & Johnson, R. (1996). *Meaningful and Manageable Assessment Through Cooperative Learning.* Edina, MN: Interaction.

Johnson, D. W., & Johnson, R. (1999). *Learning together and alone: Cooperative, competitive, and individualistic learning* (5th ed.). Boston: Allyn & Bacon.

Johnson, D. W., & Johnson, R. (2002). *Meaningful assessment: A manageable and cooperative process.* Boston: Allyn & Bacon.

Johnson, D. W., Johnson, R., & Holubec, E. (1994). *Nuts and bolts of cooperative learning.* Edina, MN: Interaction.

Johnson, D. W., Johnson, R., & Holubec, E. (1998a). *Advanced cooperative learning* (3rd ed.). Edina, MN: Interaction.

Johnson, D. W., Johnson, R., & Holubec, E. (1998b). *Cooperation in the classroom* (6th ed.). Edina, MN: Interaction.

Johnson, D. W., Johnson, R., & Johnson, F. (1976). Promoting constructive conflict in the classroom. *Notre Dame Journal of Education, 7,* 163-168.

Johnson, D. W., Johnson, R., & Smith, K. (1998). *Active learning: Cooperation in the college classroom* (2nd ed.). Edina, MN: Interaction.

Karau, D., & Williams, K. (1993). Social loafing: A meta-analytic review and theoretical integration. *Journal of Personality and Social Psychology, 65,* 681-706.

Katzenbach, J., & Smith, D. (1993). *The wisdom of teams.* Cambridge, MA: Harvard Business School Press.

Kruger, J., & Dunning, D. (1999). Unskilled and unaware of it: How difficulties in recognizing one's own incompetence lead to inflated self-assessments. *Journal of Personality and Social Psychology 77*(6), 1121-1134.

Lejk, M., Wyvill, M., & Farrow, S. (1996). A survey of methods of deriving individual grades from group assessments. *Assessment and Evaluation in Higher Education, 231,* 267-280.

Manstead, A., & Hewstone, M. (Eds.). (1995). *The Blackwell encyclopedia of social psychology.* Oxford: Blackwell.

Marrow, A. (1969). *The practical theorist: The life and work of Kurt Lewin.* New York: Basic Books.

Marwell, G., & Schmidt, D. (1975). *Cooperation: An experimental analysis.* New York: Academic Press.

Montagu, A. (1966). *On being human.* New York: Hawthorn.

Morahan-Martin, J. (1996). Should peers' evaluations be used in class projects? Questions regarding reliability, leniency, and acceptance. *Psychological Reports, 78,* 1243-1250.

Osgood, C., Suci, C., & Tannenbaum, P. (1957). *The measurement of meaning.* Urbana: University of Illinois Press.

Pearce, J. (2001). *Tolkien: Man and myth.* New York: Midpoint.

Sharan, S., & Hertz-Lazarowitz, R. (1981). A group-investigation method of cooperative learning in the classroom. In S. Sharan et al., (eds.), *Cooperation in education.* Provo, UT: Brigham Young University Press.

Sharan, S., & Sharan, Y. (1976). *Small-group teaching.* Englewood Cliffs, NJ: Educational Technology Publications.

Short, K., & Burke, C. (1991). *Creating curriculum: Teachers and students as a community of learners.* Portsmouth, NH: Heinemann.

Smith, K. (1998). Grading cooperative projects. *New Directions for Teaching and Learning, 74,* 59-67.

Sternberg, R., & Grigorenko, E. (2000, February). The myth of the lone ranger in psychological research. *American Psychological Society Observer, 11,* 27.

Swain, M., & Swaim, S. (1999). Teacher time. *Amercian Educator, 23*(3), 1-6.

Sweedler-Brown, C. (1992). The effect of training on the appearance bias of holistic essay graders. *Journal of Research and Development in Education, 26*(1), 24-29.

Terwilliger, J. (1971). *Assigning grades to students.* Glenview, IL: Scott, Foresman.

Thoits, P. (1995). Stress, coping, and social support processes: Where are we? What next? *Journal of Health and Social Behavior (extra issue)* 53–79.

Watson, J. D. (1968). *The double helix.* New York: Atheneum.

Wheeler, R., & Ryan, F. (1973). Effects of cooperative and competitive classroom environments on the attitudes and achievement of elementary school students engaged in social studies inquiry activities. *Journal of Educational Psychology, 65,* 402-407.

Wodarski, J., Hamblin, R., Buckholdt, D., & Ferritor, D. (1973). Individual consequences versus different shared consequences contingent on the performance of low-achieving members. *Journal of Applied Social Psychology, 3*(3), 276-290.

Zajonc, R. (1980). Compresence. In P. Paulus (Ed.), *Psychology of group influence* (pp. 35-60). Hillsdale, NJ: Erlbaum.

Index

CORWIN PRESS

The Corwin Press logo—a raven striding across an open book—represents the union of courage and learning. Corwin Press is committed to improving education for all learners by publishing books and other professional development resources for those serving the field of K–12 education. By providing practical, hands-on materials, Corwin Press continues to carry out the promise of its motto: **"Helping Educators Do Their Work Better."**